"Mary Hunt speaks my language in *The Financially Confident Woman*. Finance is one area where I once felt totally overwhelmed. I was anything *but* confident. But here comes Mary, with her practical advice and friendly approach, and suddenly finances became something I could not only face but conquer. There is nothing stuffy or 'textbookish' about Mary's help. She takes you by the hand, sits by your side, and helps you develop confidence you never knew you had when it comes to money. If money had a 'secret sauce,' then Mary has discovered it, and fortunately for all of us, she's serving it up with love!"

—**Hannah Keeley**, host of the TV show *Hannah, Help Me*,
founder of Mom Mastery University

"*The Financially Confident Woman* has affected my life more than any other self-help book. I read it nearly ten years ago, and for the first time in my life I understood how I needed to manage my money. I am now debt free, giving, saving, investing, and prepared for the future. I am thrilled to give my heartfelt endorsement for this revised and updated edition."

—**Kaye Pentley**

"I love this book, *The Financially Confident Woman*. It spoke to me in ways other books on the matter of money management never did. Read it. It could just change your life too."

—**Jeanette Timbre**

THE
FINANCIALLY
CONFIDENT
WOMAN

THE FINANCIALLY CONFIDENT WOMAN

What You Need to Know to Take Charge of Your Money

Mary Hunt

Revell
a division of Baker Publishing Group
Grand Rapids, Michigan

© 1996, 2015 by Mary Hunt

Published by Revell
a division of Baker Publishing Group
P.O. Box 6287, Grand Rapids, MI 49516-6287
www.revellbooks.com

Printed in the United States of America

Library of Congress Cataloging-in-Publication Data
Hunt, Mary, 1948–
    The financially confident woman : what you need to know to take charge of your money / Mary Hunt.
        pages cm
    Includes bibliographical references.
    ISBN 978-0-8007-2146-6 (pbk.)
    1. Women—Finance, Personal. 2. Saving and investment. 3. Finance, Personal—Religious aspects—Christianity. I. Title.
HG179.H855 2015
332.0240082—dc23   2014024375

Scripture quotations are from the Contemporary English Version © 1991, 1992, 1995 by American Bible Society. Used by permission.

15 16 17 18 19 20 21   7 6 5 4 3 2 1

In keeping with biblical principles of creation stewardship, Baker Publishing Group advocates the responsible use of our natural resources. As a member of the Green Press Initiative, our company uses recycled paper when possible. The text paper of this book is composed in part of post-consumer waste.

To
Posy Lough,
a confident woman I am blessed to call my friend,
colleague, and mentor

Contents

Acknowledgments

Love and support are two things of which I am particularly fond. For giving them to me, I want to thank my staff at Debt-Proof Living; my Friday night support group, Jan, Mark, and Rosalie; my editor, Vicki Crumpton; and last and most important, my husband, Harold, and my family, Jeremy and Tawny, Josh, Wendy, and Eli. I could never do this without all of you.

Introduction

It was my junior year of high school, second semester. I was down to the wire and in desperate need of just one more elective to fill my class schedule. Any class that promised an easy A would do. Little did I know that my decision would go on to become a defining moment in my life.

Imagine spending three hours a week in a dreary classroom with a teacher who does not allow the lights to be turned on—a teacher with all the personality of a dial tone who drones on and on about a subject that is so painfully boring you pray for a sudden attack of the stomach flu as a way to escape.

Welcome to beginning bookkeeping.

I barely made it out of that class with a passing grade and then only because I showed up for every class. The whole thing was one big, unintelligible blur. The teacher spoke a different language—one he forgot to teach to his students. I didn't know a debit from a credit on the first day of class or the last day either.

What I taught myself was that I could not understand anything about money and finance, and I had no plans to try to overcome this situation in the future.

I know now that the problem wasn't my inability to learn. The problem was that on the first day of class I lost my confidence. As long as I believed I could not learn this subject, I was a lost cause. And every day of that long semester I reconfirmed my belief, right through the torturous final exam. From that day on I would avoid anything having to do with accounting, balance sheets, accounting records, and the dreaded reconciliation. I lumped all money management under the dreadful heading "bookkeeping."

I know now that the words I spoke to myself turned into my thoughts. Every thought was imposed on my subconscious and emerged as an attitude. Those words became powerful in my life. I had an aversion to anything having to do with numbers. What I believed became a self-fulfilling prophecy. Without confidence that I could learn and understand how to manage money—both in deed and on paper—I was exactly what I believed: a money idiot.

For much of my life after that disastrous bookkeeping class, I lived under a dark cloud of worry that I would become financially destitute and homeless. I worried that eventually I'd find myself living under a bridge. As irrational as that might seem, according to a recent survey, I'm not the only one who's ever had such a thought. Nearly 50 percent of women in the US admit they are financially insecure and worry about that bag lady thing.[1]

Ladies, we need to talk. We don't have to accept financial insecurity as some kind of life sentence. And that constant and gnawing fear of becoming destitute? Forget it! We can do something about this.

We were created uniquely to birth children, organize households, resolve problems, run companies, and effect change in the world. Why do we struggle when it comes to this matter of money? It's not for a lack of intelligence. The problem is that we lack confidence. We're not sure where to start, whom to ask, or what to do.

Financial confidence is a choice. It's a matter of learning simple financial principles, then consciously applying them over and over again until they become automatic responses—financial habits.

No matter how crazy you've been with money, I'm pretty sure I've got you beat. And I have it on very good authority that with God's power you can change. I hope that makes you excited about the future, makes you stop throwing away your bank statements, and gives you confidence that you can live the title of this book. At the very least, I hope you don't regret buying it.

My journey into the credit card abyss began quite innocently. I would never have considered my behavior irresponsible. I was simply agreeing to have it all now and pay for it later. I was pushing the envelope, living on the edge, and going for the gusto because I would go around only once (obviously every marketing genius dreams of a consumer like me). Throwing caution to the wind and living spontaneously were my definitions of enjoying life.

Me, irresponsible? No way! I was progressive, inventive, and creative. The challenge was that in order to carry off this persona I needed money, lots of it, and more than I happened to have at the time. I was driven to find new and better ways to mortgage my future; otherwise, I might be forced to stifle my marvelously whimsical tendencies and sudden inspirations.

I learned the hard way that irresponsible financial behavior eventually brings financial devastation. Activities meant to make me soar clipped my wings instead and sent me hurling into a pit of despair. My plan for freedom became my own prescription for bondage.

Financially irresponsible people are not bad people. They've developed bad habits—habits of omission, habits based on what our gotta-get-it-all-right-now, credit-crazed society insists is normal. They've chosen to get their financial "education" from the consumer credit industry, which wants them to be in debt until the day they die. Because they've never been educated on matters of personal finance, they don't know when they're making mistakes; therefore, they don't learn from those mistakes until it's too late. The good news is that bad habits can be unlearned and good habits learned. Having a desire to change is the key to becoming financially responsible.

If you are searching for quick fixes or ways to manipulate your present situation so you can qualify for more debt, this is not the book for you. However, if you're tired of always being broke, feel you cannot handle another monthly bill, are fresh out of juggling techniques, and fear things might never change, I'm glad we've found each other.

This is not a book about how to get more money. It's about how to become financially confident by learning how to manage what you already have. It's not a book equating poverty with spirituality. It's a book about right living, abundance, joy, and the peace of mind that results from financial confidence.

This is not an exhaustive treatment of the entire subject of personal finance and money management. That would not be a book—it would be a set of books and heavy ones at that. I have taken the basic things you need to know and boiled them down, giving you what you need to know to become financially confident.

In encouraging you to look deep into your personal belief system, I've had to come to a screeching halt on more than one occasion and search my own heart—that secret place deep within from which come my own attitudes and values. It continues to be a humbling experience, as I realize that only as I'm willing to be changed can I help others do the same.

I have so much to tell you, and I pray the information will change your life the way it has mine. No matter where you are on the spectrum of financial responsibility, I have something wonderful to offer you—hope, confidence, and peace.

PART 1

SELF-
EXAMINATION

1

Confessions of a Financially Irresponsible Woman

When money talks, it often says "good-bye."
anonymous, quoted in
Poor Richard Jr.'s Almanac

I had my first taste of freedom when I left home in Spokane, Washington, to attend college in California. I'll never forget my first week in Los Angeles. Like my first kiss, it was better than I'd ever dreamed, and, quite frankly, I wished it could last forever. The beautiful weather, the palm trees, the lights, and the excitement of the big city were far beyond anything I'd ever imagined. I just knew that college would be my paradise on earth.

I intended to waste no time fulfilling my childhood promise: When I grew up, I'd be rich. You see, I mistakenly equated my constant feelings of sadness with the fact that I felt poor. It made perfect sense to me that being rich would produce happiness, and I just couldn't wait to be happy.

As California's newest Cinderella, I had been planning this transition from poor to rich for a long time. The moment I set foot on campus, my dream ceased being a fantasy and became a self-fulfilling prophecy.

I wasted no time opening a checking account. I knew I would need one to keep my money safe. I had a vague idea about how checking accounts worked. After all, I did take high school bookkeeping, painful as that experience was. And I must say that I was surprised that, contrary to my preconceived notions, this device appeared to be simple and quite user-friendly. But I didn't know my checkbook carried a hidden danger.

The first time the idea crept into my mind I was with a group of friends—friends with cars and freeway savvy who introduced me to the world of California shopping malls. The idea of writing checks with no money in the account was about as insane an idea as I'd ever had. Even I knew that was not in keeping with acceptable accounting principles. I halfheartedly pushed the idea out of the way. And seconds later the idea returned.

The more I thought about it, the less outrageous it seemed. After all, who'd know? No one, not even the salesclerk, could know exactly how much money I had in my account. I could buy the things I wanted and, as a bonus, impress my friends with my fiscal prowess. Given sufficient time to get used to the concept—about thirty seconds—I didn't think my idea was so insane after all; I'd do it just this once.

Unfortunately, my crazy idea worked quite well. Not only were my friends impressed with my ability to keep up with them (they didn't come right out and say it, but I knew), but the salesperson also had to have been surprised by my ability to buy whatever I wanted. Acting rich gave me a sense of significance and, in turn, a fabulous feeling.

I figured out how to shop on Wednesday, get paid from my college library job on Friday, deposit the check on Monday, and have time to spare to cover the checks I'd written. Nobody was harmed because no one knew the difference. It was exciting too because it felt like I was getting away with something—beating the system. Taking this kind of risk was exhilarating in some crazy way.

I didn't see what I was doing as wrong; I was simply being creative in my efforts to keep up the lifestyle to which I was becoming increasingly accustomed. Even when I bounced checks, I didn't question the procedure I'd discovered. I was pretty easy on myself, concluding I wasn't exactly overdrawn, just under-deposited.

My checking account escapades were the start of a destructive habit I allowed to take root in my life: I habitually engaged in the activity of acquiring first and figuring out how to pay later.

Somehow I made it through college without being subjected to public humiliation for having accounts closed due to excessive overdrafts. I escaped being arrested for kiting (the illegal practice of writing a bad check on one account to cover an overdraft on another).

I have no idea how much money I spent on insufficient funds fees, but it had to have been a lot. Still, I refused to see my financial behavior as irresponsible or self-destructive. After all, like many college students, I'd just spent the better part of four years being financially strapped. My creativity allowed me to spend what I didn't have at the moment to get what I couldn't live without. It was no big deal, and I didn't plan to do it forever.

When I married Harold shortly after graduation, I assumed that I'd never have to worry about money again. After all, I'd grown up believing that a man was supposed to take care of his wife, handle the finances, and make sure that she, whose job it was to spend the money, had plenty of it. And this was no ordinary man. I married a banker.

In the absence of any counseling to the contrary, I figured that Harold would make loads of money and I'd create a lovely

21

lifestyle for us. However, in hindsight, the fact that I insisted we needed a credit card (just in case of an emergency, of course) is clear evidence that deep inside I didn't feel he could handle his financial responsibilities and needed my intervention.

Plastic Significance

The arrival of my first credit card triggered another insane idea in my head. I found that using a gasoline credit card was far superior to spending the cash I might have in my wallet. It was easier to use plastic at the corner gas station. But the idea that went off in my head was far more dangerous than that of mere convenience. It shouted, "We get free gas whenever we want it!" Not having to worry about whether I had enough cash to pay for gasoline and choosing "full serve" to boot made me feel rich, dignified, and significant. My contact with rich people had been limited, so the way they behaved was pretty much left up to my imagination. And I had one terrific imagination!

As a young girl, I was blessed with a best friend, Judy. As a bonus to our friendship, Judy's parents were the richest people I'd ever known. They had a beautiful home and contemporary furnishings. Judy's dad had a telephone in his car, and her mom owned a successful business. Judy had what I understood to be unlimited access to her mother's accounts at all kinds of stores, not the least of which was the little corner grocery store.

Whenever I stayed over at Judy's—which was as often as I could finagle parental permission—I too became a rich kid. I was treated with the same privilege, love, and respect as a member of the Ellis family. I had acceptance and approval.

Judy and I had great freedom, which included unlimited entitlement to the little corner grocery store. We could buy anything we wanted anytime we felt like it. Anything. And we never needed money. The store owner, Rawley, made us feel like the most important girls in the world. Armed with Judy's signature alone, we could be on our way with the best selection of groceries any two teenagers could imagine. There were no limitations and no accountability—at least that was my perception.

I wonder now what kind of conversations resulted when Mrs. Ellis received that monthly bill. But for me that part of the story didn't exist. I just assumed that, because they were rich, eventual payment was just taken care of the same way a princess is taken care of. It just happens.

I lived for the weekends when I could experience firsthand the delights and freedom of being rich. To this day, some of my fondest memories involve stayovers at Judy's house, where I received my first taste of significance and individual importance. It's no wonder I associated those wonderful feelings with money.

Fast-forward to that first gasoline card. As you might imagine, the initial excitement of gasoline entitlement wore off quickly when the monthly statement arrived. Surely someone had made a mistake. There's no way we'd filled up that many times. And the worst part? The gasoline company wanted full payment immediately. It was clear to me that we needed another brand of gasoline credit card to spread the purchases around. Then another and another.

Soon after, while I strolled through a local department store, a salesperson invited me to apply for the store's credit card. All I needed to qualify was a valid credit card, and my gasoline card would do. Talk about too good to be true! Of course I accepted with no regrets because once again I felt I was doing something noble—preparing for emergencies. Within just a few minutes, I was entitled to a lot more than just gasoline.

This revolving credit idea was really getting into my blood. It seemed so workable, so logical. A two-hundred-dollar purchase wasn't that at all. It was merely a ten-dollar monthly payment. Highly affordable in my book.

Of course, intellectually, I'm sure I knew better, but my ability to slip into denial transcended reason. I was able to remain comfortable because of my unique ability to justify and defend my activities.

My Plastic Safety Net

It didn't take long for me to get caught up in the excitement of credit card acquisitions. I was like a kid working on a baseball card collection. I never intended to use them, just to have these lines of credit in place in case of an emergency. To me, they were like seat belts, a first-aid kit, jumper cables, and oat bran all rolled into one neat little package. I was convinced that my credit cards would protect, nourish, comfort, and cure.

I had many "emergencies" during the following years and felt fully entitled to meet those needs using plastic. What I believed about them was absolutely true. They worked like a charm to relieve pain and worry. They offered asylum from the penalties of past-due property taxes and provided wonderful Christmas holidays for our two boys and extended families. Even the dentist and preschool accepted plastic. Credit cards worked perfectly in bridging the gap between what I'd determined was our woefully inadequate income and the cost of maintaining the minimum acceptable lifestyle—a lifestyle that demanded I provide for our two little boys, Jeremy and Josh, all the things I'd missed during my childhood.

Just when I thought it couldn't get any better, several of our credit card companies offered that glorious added feature: the cash advance. Even though plastic was accepted nearly everywhere, there were occasions when I needed plain old green stuff, and the cash advance came to the rescue.

Because we kept up with the monthly payments and incurred a minimal number of late fees, we were fairly well qualified to land new forms of credit. I knew how the applications needed to read in order to be approved.

Because our credit report was pretty clean and Harold had an excellent job with a large California bank, credit wasn't the only thing we could acquire. We were able to purchase a home in a location where home values were escalating at an unprecedented rate. Our home in Orange County was increasing in value by at least 20 percent a year. At this rate, our three-bedroom house would be worth $5 million or even $10 million by the time we wanted to think about retirement. There was no need to start a savings program or plan for the future. When the time came, we'd put out a for-sale sign, sell the house quickly, gather up our millions, and sail off into the retirement sunset. I had it all figured out.

Because I'd gotten into the habit of always spending more money than we had available, on quite a few occasions we had to refinance and take out second and even third mortgages on the house. After all, we had to eat. With each new loan came another payment and a greater necessity to find new sources of income. Of course, each time we refinanced I promised Harold that we'd pay off the debts and stop using credit as soon as we got things straightened out or after this thing or that thing happened.

But things never straightened out—for a million reasons, not the least of which was because we were young and figured we'd have plenty of time to save when our income increased. Unfortunately, as the years passed, our financial obligations increased at a greater pace than our income.

Meltdown

After we'd been married for about twelve years, the minimum monthly payments on all our debts reached an amount dangerously close to our take-home pay. Most of our credit card credit lines were at the max, and juggling was a way of life. It was not unusual for us to use the next month's check to cover this month's bills or to pay half the bills this month and half the next. We were constantly chasing new forms of credit to stay afloat.

I convinced my banker husband that his occupation would never cut it income-wise and that we should consider self-employment. It seemed like a good idea to me. Self-employed people, so I thought, were smart and wealthy. Self-employment would allow us to make the amount of money we needed. Harold wasn't all that enamored with the future the bank seemed to be offering and detested the politics he was being pressured to play. The banking industry was facing major revamping, and the idea of a new challenge and the bright hope of self-employment became attractive to both of us. We had dreams to fulfill and children to raise. We wanted a bright and inviting future, not one plagued with a constant shortage of money.

Once we opened our minds to such a drastic employment change, we became giant magnets to the many "opportunities" that existed. Harold had befriended a couple of his bank clients, and both of us couldn't help but be fascinated by their new German-made sports cars and very large daily cash deposits. We were entertained in their Newport Beach homes, and their lifestyles really turned our heads. It didn't take long for their casual interest in us to become more deliberate. We were being sought after to join them in their mega-enterprise. They didn't pressure us. They simply befriended us and allowed us to view the good life. We checked the organization out as well as we could; however, our minds were already made up. I'm sure we were blind to warning signs that must have been screaming out to us.

We went to Atlanta as honored guests at the organization's annual sales meeting. Imagine how significant we felt as our friends, who had made their way high into the organization, introduced the banker who'd caught this marvelous organization's vision and was leaving sixteen years of tenure to become the newest company owner.

As thousands of people cheered, the entire episode was videotaped. I remember thinking how wonderful it was to have this momentous occasion recorded for our family's history and generations to come. I could see myself slipping behind the steering wheel of my own German-made sports car. I was so proud, so optimistic, and so happy for my husband, who'd finally made a very difficult decision to leave his comfort zone and take an exciting risk.

Our trip back to California was energized by our resolve to be excellent employers and worthy stewards of this magnanimous new wealth that was about to be thrust upon us. Our plans were set, and we wasted no time putting them into action.

Harold gave his resignation and customary notice to the bank, and we figured out how we could borrow the thousands of dollars we'd need to get into the business. A short-term loan was all we needed because this particular business was cash intensive. Repayment would be swift and sure.

Of course, we needed a site for the business. (Did I mention it involved reselling poor-quality merchandise? I mean very poor quality—so awful, in fact, that this stuff would hardly have a chance of moving at a garage sale.) Since I'd dabbled in industrial real estate, I was able to pull off a lease and even earn a commission. Next, we needed to furnish the place. We rented office furnishings and accessories. One tenet of corporate headquarters was that each franchise needed to have a look of success to attract the caliber of people who would make sure success happened.

We worked hard, but it was clear almost from the start that we'd been terribly misled about how easy it was going to be to get up and running profitably in a short time. Every cent we had borrowed plus every additional dollar we could rake off our credit card limits were poured into the business. We felt we'd already put so much in that we had to protect the initial investment. We justified letting our personal bills slide for a few months because we were still convinced the cash would start flowing. Then we'd get everything caught up and be none the worse for the temporary delay.

About two months into this self-employment nightmare, I grew fearful. The honeymoon was over, and the tension was setting in. We weren't able to hire all the people we needed in spite of very expensive advertising. Our furniture and warehouse rental payments were much larger than they had seemed when we signed the paperwork. It was clear we were undercapitalized and overly optimistic.

And those two wonderful men who'd introduced us to our dream of a lifetime? They were gone and have remained gone to this day. Clearly their automobiles and homes were rented short-term to allow them to come into the area, fleece every sucker they could find, and leave before anyone could catch up with them. They were clever too. We had nothing with which we could prove fraud or deception.

It took four months for our business to go from start to finish, the longest four months of our lives. We experienced every emotion of which we were capable, usually all at once.

As our hopes and dreams were being dashed, so was our relationship. Things hadn't been terrific between us for quite a long time before this self-employment episode, but we had passed it off as the financial strain we were under, my unwillingness to spend less, and my insistence that he earn more. This new dream business had given us a common goal, and it had temporarily rekindled our marriage.

It took four months for our dream to die. We buried it the day all the rented furniture was repossessed and we walked away from the building. It was a painful and torturous death, and with it something in both of us died. Harold had gone from tenured bank employee to future millionaire to unemployed business owner in about sixteen weeks. To make matters worse, he had no unemployment benefits. Our income was zero, our home was moving closer to foreclosure each day, and we were defenseless against the pit of despair into which we were slipping. We had no idea what to do. When we needed each other the most, we were the least able to communicate or to reach out to each other. We were two angry individuals completely isolated in our pain.

I cannot remember a time before or since when I have felt such utter defeat, pain, anger, and debilitating fear. When faced with life's challenges, I had always had a plan B, another idea, an alternative. My controlling temperament had always pulled me through, but I was completely unable to rescue this situation. We had bills on top of bills, debts to the ceiling, and, most seriously, we were in danger of losing our home.

And Then God . . .

It was September 1982. We'd just lost the business. I was paralyzed by fear and pain like I'd never known. I was fresh out of ideas. When I reached the end of myself and ran out of schemes and solutions, God was able to get my attention.

I grew up in church, graduated from a Christian college, married a committed Christian, and was very active in church. The problem was that I'd never allowed God to invade my life. I kept him compartmentalized. My Christianity was convenient on Sundays or when missionaries visited. But when it came to my day-to-day life, I had it figured out. I found security and dignity in the color and quantity of my credit cards and in my ability to borrow money. Now my house of cards was collapsing around me.

It was as if God turned on the floodlights of heaven, and for the first time I was able to acknowledge what I'd done. I saw

29

what a horrible mess I'd made and what I'd done to my husband, my family, and myself.

Completely broken, I confessed that the manipulation, scheming, deceit, and lying were sin. I begged for God's forgiveness (which, of course, was mine for the asking). I pleaded with God to let me keep my husband, my kids, and our home. I promised God on that day that I would do anything and everything necessary to pay back all the debt, change my ways, and find my security only in him. Of course, God forgave me the instant I sought forgiveness. All the debts were not mysteriously repaid or wiped forever from the records of all the companies and individuals to whom we owed money. And my pain did not immediately disappear. But God forgave me.

I spent the next twelve years working hard and learning everything I could about myself. God marvelously provided a job for me—a real estate position in which I was able to earn a regular salary as well as commissions. We learned how to cut expenses and live without incurring new debt. There were occasions when we were slow learners, and we didn't do everything perfectly. But the point is this: As I was willing to change, God made those changes possible.

The ways God provided and taught me are probably another book in themselves. But let me make this point absolutely clear: I allowed terrible habits to guide my life—actions I practiced habitually until they became almost automatic. Those habits when practiced over a long period of time had an accumulative, devastating effect.

Time to Pay Up

It took thirteen years, but we paid back the entire $100,000 in unsecured debt, plus all the interest and associated fees. We did not stiff one creditor for a single dime. We asked for no concessions and expected no discounts. I came face-to-face with my compulsive overspending problem and learned one day at a time how to deal with it and how to depend on God to meet our needs instead of looking to credit as the solution.

As we've obeyed God's financial principles of giving, saving, and not spending more than we have, he's blessed us in ways we could never have imagined. The irony is that now I have the wonderful privilege of helping people all over the country apply these same principles to their lives, get out of debt, and learn how to joyfully live beneath their means. It is possible to become responsible in areas where irresponsibility has been the order of the day.

I have not had a personality transplant. I'm still me. I will always have compulsive tendencies. All these years later, I'm still learning how to control my compulsive nature and maintain good financial habits. During those twenty-five years, the years when we should have been preparing for the future by saving and investing, we were doing just the opposite. We've had to work doubly hard to make up for lost time. But wonderful things have happened since the day I hit bottom, and I am so grateful.

PART 2

ROLES, MYTHS, AND REFORMATION

2

Where Is It Written
"Women Don't Do Money"?

Human beings, by changing the inner attitudes of
their minds, can change the outer aspects of their lives.

William James

Lucy Ricardo taught me that being dumber than dirt is kind
of cute. Her neighbor Ethel was a little smarter but only occasionally managed to overcome Lucy's dumbness. And Gracie
Allen (remember her?). Well, she was dumber than Lucy and
Ethel put together.

Those women could certainly spend the money, couldn't they?
Thank goodness for Ricky, Fred, and George. Where would
those women have been without the men to take care of them,
protect them from themselves, and pay all the bills?

Those television husbands always managed to clean up their
wives' messes. It didn't matter to what degree Lucy's own toxicity
overwhelmed her; Ricky always had the solution and just in the
nick of time. The women never had to think about money, and

they didn't care much about where it came from as long as it kept coming. I guess the men worked—that part of the plot was always a little foggy for me. Ricky left every morning for rehearsal; Fred hung out and collected rent. And George Burns? I haven't a clue what he did for a living. I don't think Gracie did either.

Those women didn't participate in the family finances, and that was the way we thought it was supposed to be. They spent their days poking into everyone's business and were consumed with how much trouble they could stir up.

The men were the protectors, the "bailer outers," and the problem solvers. Of course, they handled all the finances. That was my favorite part. It was so romantic to be a bit helpless and silly. The secret was having a smart husband with unlimited sources of money who would always take care of everything.

Waiting for Prince Charming

As a little girl, I got the message that being protected and loved meant never having to know about money. In my world, women took care of the relationships and men took care of the money. Women were the emotional caretakers, men the wage earners.

I learned that men go to work, women shop and spend, and no one ever talks about it. My mother didn't handle any money. She had what she called "pin money," but it was not considered essential to her financial well-being or that of our family.

I learned that a good husband was measured by his ability to be a good provider, which meant he earned the money, paid the bills, and made all the financial decisions. I didn't learn appropriate and useful money skills because handling money was the exclusive territory of men. By default, I learned that "women don't do money."

No wonder I breathed a big sigh of relief as I walked down the aisle. Not only was I marrying a terrific guy, but I would also no longer have to worry about "man stuff," like car trouble and money, because I'd found my provider, my caretaker, my man. I'd take care of the woman things, and he'd do the man things. We never actually talked about it. Some things didn't require discussion.

You know where this kind of flawed thinking got me. Let's put it this way: I didn't find marriage to be one lively episode after another of *I Love Lucy*. My shenanigans with money weren't solved in thirty-minute segments, complete with laugh track. I didn't get a bailout and a fresh start every day as credits rolled and the theme music played.

Distinctly Different

I do believe men and women are distinct creations.

As women, we want happiness, we want significance, and we want to receive respect and honor from men. We want to feel that we have a genuine purpose in life. We want to receive joy and satisfaction from our work, whether that work is in the home, outside the home, or both. We want to feel secure, and we also want to feel valued for our intelligence and management abilities.

Personally, I believe some men use control of family finances as a way to keep their wives dependent and subordinate. Please don't misunderstand me. I can't think of a more noble calling than to be a wife and mother. I'm not suggesting for a moment that every woman must leave the home and join the working world. Nor am I suggesting that every woman must marry in order to be fulfilled and live a meaningful life. And I'm not saying that women should control the family purse. What I am saying is this: Every woman, regardless of her marital status, age, strengths, or weaknesses, needs to know how to manage money confidently and effectively.

37

A Peek inside the Mailbag

I get a lot of mail (and when I say a lot, I mean file drawers full of snail mail and email too) from men and women, old and young, from every state and many foreign countries. These people are, for the most part, readers of *Debt-Proof Living*, a newsletter I write and have published since 1992 (shameless plug).

Many of these letters start out, "Dear Mary, What I'm about to tell you I've never told another soul. . . ." I'd estimate that about 85 percent of the letters I receive are from women, and of that number at least 50 percent are from women in pain who tell me of their frustration and struggles with money. I've learned so much about myself and others through this unique form of education. Take a peek into my files:

I'm so discouraged. No matter how hard I try, there's never enough money. I just don't know what to do.

I've tried to save, but every time I put some money away, something comes up. Right now I have $1,100 in bills I can't pay. The creditors are calling, and I'm terrified.

I'm a housewife with three girls. We live paycheck to paycheck. My husband refuses to admit just how bad things really are. I have no idea where his paycheck goes. If only I knew someone to lend us some money.

I feel as if I am sinking in an abyss of financial ignorance.

My heart is so heavy. . . . I hate myself when I fail over and over. I was doing so good at not using plastic but have fallen off the wagon again. We are at least $1,000 short every month, and I am dying inside.

We're always in some crisis about money, but my husband just ignores it. I just don't know where the money goes.

He is a good provider most of the time, but during the slow months it's really terrible. I worry so much about money I'm making myself sick.

I've always wanted to buy a home, but I think that will never happen. My husband left me with the kids and all the bills.

When he died, I was shocked to find out the condition of our finances. For forty-eight years I had no idea what was going on because he always handled the money.

I'm so sick of always being broke and having to pretend that everything is okay.

If I have it, I spend it. It's like I can't help myself. For me, going shopping is like playing roulette. I just never know what's going to happen.

Money is just too hard for me. I feel like a failure.

I only wish I had the ability to earn more money. Things are very tough, and I just don't know how we'll make it.

I hope you can help me. I'm all alone for the first time in twenty-eight years. I don't even know where to start.

I thought the insurance money would be plenty. I realize now that I should have looked for someone to tell me how to invest it. Between lending it to the kids and fixing up the house, it's just about gone, and I have no idea what I'll do when it is.

These women have reached a critical point. They need the skills and the knowledge to competently manage money, but they don't know what to do to take control. Their situations are controlling them, and that is a terrible place to be.

Maybe you too have felt some of the same painful, frustrating, discouraging, hopeless, and scary feelings. Perhaps you've secretly wondered, What's the matter with me? I can't control my spending, and I feel anxious and frustrated about money. I have no one to take care of me, and I don't know what I'm doing. I'm afraid something terrible is going to happen.

Fiscal Reality

A woman who has never been exposed to the subject of money management is typically afraid of making financial decisions. She doesn't feel capable and doesn't feel she can trust herself to make these kinds of decisions. She'd just as soon have someone else make all the financial decisions for her. I say this because it was true for me. Don't make me think! Just tell me what to do. Have you ever thought those words—or said them out loud?

You might believe that money is not an important concern because you have a husband to make it, handle it, and manage it. Perhaps you are a young woman still living at home, waiting for Prince Charming to show up on his white horse with a promise that you will never have to worry your pretty little head about a thing.

Listen. You have to look beyond today. Chances are great that sometime during your lifetime things will change. You will be required to skillfully manage money, and you might not have a great deal of warning.

There's also the distinct probability that if you are married your husband would love for you to start participating as a partner in the money area of your lives. For those of you who have children, consider what a terrific parenting team you and your husband make. The same could happen in your financial life.

Money-Conscious Women

Greater numbers of women are becoming money conscious because women are managing more money than ever before. More women are reaching top positions in the workplace. We are enjoying better female earning capacity and a highly educated female population. In fact, women control 60 percent of the wealth in the United States.[1] Yet despite all they have achieved, women still feel financially insecure. Want to know just how insecure?

Forty-seven percent of women who participated in a 2013 "Women, Money, and Power Study,"[2] commissioned by Allianz Insurance, said they feel very insecure about money and worry about ending up destitute—they fear becoming bag ladies. And this even applied to those women who are considered high-income earners, making more than $200,000 annually.

Most women when surveyed say they will depend on Social Security to be their primary source of income during their golden years.[3] Currently, the average monthly Social Security payment is $1,269.[4] Could you make it on that income alone? Probably not, given that the average non-mortgage debt for a woman in the United States is $25,095.[5]

Seventy-two percent of women say retirement is their primary investment goal, yet nearly half (48 percent) do not participate in a retirement savings plan, and 60 percent have not taken the necessary steps to prepare for retirement. Here's another shocker: Men save over 75 percent more over a lifetime than women do.[6]

In addition, according to the Administration on Aging, the following is true[7]:

- Nearly 73 percent of all older persons living alone are women.
- More than 70 percent of all elderly persons with incomes below the poverty level are women.
- Fifty percent of women who married within the last twenty years will divorce. Ten percent will remain single.

You have a nine out of ten chance that at some point in your life you will be solely responsible for your own financial situation.[8]

41

Will you know what to do then? That will depend a great deal on what you are doing now.

Whether you are currently using them or not, you need to keep up your skills and your education so that in the event of a major life change you will have the confidence necessary to deal with it.

While it is slowly closing, the wage gap still exists in this country. Women earn seventy-seven cents for every dollar earned by men.[9] That alone is a good argument for why women, above all, need to possess excellent financial planning and management skills. According to Wells Fargo, 70 percent of women with a written plan for how to manage their finances are confident they will have enough saved for their retirement (compared to 44 percent for those without a plan).[10]

Whether you are solely responsible for your financial well-being, you share it with your partner, or you want to be prepared for any eventuality, there's no time like the present to start learning how to become a financially confident woman. A wife who says, "My husband handles that sort of thing," is likely giving away a huge part of her life.

The traditional arrangement in which the wife is not involved in the family finances (being given money each week for groceries and household expenses doesn't count as being involved in the family finances) is not only shortsighted but also plain toxic. The other extreme, in which the husband opts out of all financial matters, leaving all the bills and financial planning to his modern wife, is no better.

Typically, one of the two partners in a marriage is more naturally gifted with numbers. Terrific! Then that person should keep the records but not make all the decisions.

Becoming more knowledgeable about money means more than just knowing how to pay the bills or balance the checkbook. It means understanding money—compounding interest, credit, debt—and how to manage it.

In my home, I am the one who's not good with numbers, so Harold manages our bank accounts. It's not that I don't know how or couldn't do it if he wasn't available. It has nothing to do with gender and everything to do with talent. When it comes to major financial decisions and the monthly bills, we review everything together and make decisions together.

The Nurturing Female

Men and women bring different things to a marriage. As a woman, I know I have God-given strengths by virtue of my female genes. I'm a nurturer. I'm more sensitive to detail and able to keep track of where things are and where they're supposed to be. I love to watch things grow. Knowing everyone is safe and tucked in at night somehow gives me a feeling of well-being and security.

God placed those characteristics inside of me, and guess what? Those parts of my personality make me the best one to look after our investments. They need to be nurtured and allowed to grow in the safest place possible. Harold and I are a team, and since we've learned to be team players in this area of personal finance, our relationship has grown tremendously, as has our financial picture.

Stop for a moment and think about how smart, clever, capable, and responsible you are in so many areas of your life. Perhaps you single-handedly run a household, possessing excellent skills as a scheduler, cleaner, chauffeur, chef, dietitian, tutor, athletic coordinator, laundress, seamstress, landscape artist, florist, purchasing agent, and nurse. Perhaps you are very successful in your career and have gained the respect of your peers in the professional world. There is absolutely no reason you cannot add money manager and financial planner to your list of abilities and skills.

Money management needs to become as important in your life as all the other skills you've learned. A financially confident woman is a woman who has the knowledge, ability, and desire to behave in a financially responsible manner. The designation is available to anyone.

Money Do's and Don'ts for Women

Do	Don't
Be a giver.	Be a taker.
Save a portion of every paycheck and other money at the time it flows into your life.	Wait to see what's left at the end of the month.
See yourself as an equal contributor to the welfare and well-being of your family.	Consider yourself a second-class partner if you don't happen to earn a paycheck.
Nurture your financial identity.	Depend on your partner or another person to make your financial decisions.
Develop and maintain skills so that you are capable of earning a living.	Let your education go to waste by allowing your job skills to become obsolete.
Communicate openly about all areas of personal financial planning.	Assume anything.
Plan ahead for emergencies.	Fool yourself by thinking challenges of a financial nature will never come to you and your family.
Take pride in your position as manager or comanager of the most important organization on earth—your family.	Ever put yourself down.
Consider debt something to be avoided if at all possible. It really is a four-letter word.	Count your credit limits as part of your income or as an entitlement to have what you cannot afford with your regular income.
Order copies of your credit reports at least annually.	Assume the credit-reporting agencies never make a mistake.

3

Responsible Is Not
Another Word for Boring

Look, managing your money is just one part of managing your life. It may not be your favorite part. But like getting dressed every morning, taking out the garbage a few times a week, and visiting the gynecologist once a year, it has to be done. It's irresponsible to do otherwise.

Jean Chatzky

At first glance, the part-time college library assistant position seemed like the perfect job for me. Since I was transportationally challenged, working on campus would have its advantages.

My interview was not idyllic, however. The college librarian was about as stereotypically stern and matronly as any casting director would want to find for such a role. She had the part down pat. She also had great intuition. Prior to hiring me as her assistant, she gave me quite a lecture on responsibility.

45

It didn't take long for me to develop a healthy fear of the woman and an equally healthy determination not to let her devotion to responsibility rub off on me. I slipped into my responsible self during work hours and shed it as quickly as possible when my time was up.

Why did the whole idea of being responsible sound so boring? To me, responsibility was what divided the dull personalities from those who had a life. In my world, responsibility was what kept the less-than-fun group hopelessly dormitory-bound. The risk takers were anything but responsible. I guess you might say irresponsibility was where the action was. It didn't take me long to decide where I wanted to be. Responsibility tied people down, so irresponsibility should free them up. Thus, my experiences with throwing caution to the wind and living for the moment began.

With that background, I find it quite amazing that this is a book about responsible living. God's willingness to redeem even the most unlikely people is something that continues to amaze me. Make no mistake, however; this is not a book about how to become matronly, boring, and dull. This is a book about financial responsibility. It is not a book about budgets. If you ask me, there are already too many books about budgets.

This is a book about the miracles that can happen when irresponsible financial habits are forever replaced with responsible ones.

Since my younger days, I have learned that it is possible to be responsible and fun-loving. It is possible to be financially mature and contemporary. It is possible to be responsible and spontaneous. Responsibility simply means being accountable, and that is a good thing.

No matter what the terms *responsible* and *irresponsible* mean to you, I hope that for the next hundred pages or so you'll be able to set aside any preconceived notions, sit back, and enjoy.

Maybe you'll learn something new. Then again, you might discover you're one of those sorts for whom financial responsibility comes naturally—and you're a fun person too. If so, your habits are what the rest of us wish to emulate. We want to be like you.

The Basic Plan

By the time you finish this book, you will have the basic tools to:

- assess your relationship with money
- take control of irresponsible behaviors
- replace them with behaviors that are responsible
- see that those positive financial behaviors become lifelong habits

First, we are going to take a quick look at how our beliefs, attitudes, and values determine how we behave with money.

Next, we will tackle the idea of how repeated behaviors become habits, whether they're positive behaviors or negative. We will see how we can choose to change an inappropriate behavior by examining the beliefs that are responsible for that behavior.

We will then identify the habits of a financially responsible woman and set out to purposely do the things she does. We will replace our bad habits with actions that are in accordance with God's Word.

The "Am I Financially Irresponsible?" Self-Diagnosis Test

Answer yes or no to the following statements.

1. I have nothing close to a reasonable knowledge of my income, fixed expenses, irregular expenses, and net worth.
2. I don't have the discipline to be good with money.
3. I am near, at, or over the limit on my credit cards.

4. I've bounced more than three checks in the past year.

5. I often use this month's income to cover last month's bills.

6. I can't imagine living without credit.

7. I've never been concerned about money because I have a spouse who takes care of it.

8. I worry about money quite a bit.

9. I hide the mail.

10. I don't have a formal savings program.

11. If I had more money, I'd be just fine.

12. I have lied to my spouse or creditors about making payments.

13. I know that giving is important, but I just don't have enough money right now.

14. I've taken a cash advance on one credit card to make the payment on another card.

If you answered no to every question, you are my hero. You are a financially responsible person. If you answered yes to one or two questions, your tendencies lean toward responsible, but you should consider these areas to be red flags. Three to five yes answers are a definite sign that you're headed for financial trouble. I hope you will soon see the need to turn around immediately. Yes on six or more? There's no doubt about it—we need each other. I recommend you not leave home until you finish this book.

4

Time Out for a
Values Inventory

Ever wonder why one person is a big spender, another is a big saver, and yet another wants to stick her head in the sand about her finances? Well, what we believe about money impacts how we handle it.

Maria Lin

What are your money beliefs? Could you articulate them if it were really important to do so? Could you write them down?

It's possible you've never even thought about your money beliefs beyond knowing that you like money and never seem to have enough. How you deal with money (your money behavior) is determined by what you think about money (your money beliefs). Your money behavior is an outward display of what you believe about money and its role in your life. If you've never thought about this before, it's likely that those beliefs are nebulous and buried somewhere in your subconscious mind.

Behaviors

Behaviors are symptoms of internal beliefs. Trying to manage symptoms while ignoring the underlying cause is a waste of time and energy. Haven't we learned that from all the diets and budgets we've tried? Sure, they might work for a day or a week, maybe longer, but in time diets and budgets fail because they just don't get down to the root of the problem.

Beliefs

A belief is a feeling of certainty about what something means. It is a statement we make about ourselves or the world. Clearly, it is possible to have personal beliefs that are not based in truth. Once a false belief is identified, it is possible for us to dump it and replace it with one that is true.

Attitudes

A group of beliefs regarding a subject produces an attitude. Once an attitude is formed, behavior regarding that subject becomes pretty much automatic.

If my attitude toward dogs is one of fear, it's quite likely I had a bad experience with a dog somewhere along the line. So every time I encounter a dog, I experience fear—an automatic response based on a group of beliefs. Each of us has a belief system that is made up of many beliefs that in turn produce many attitudes.

Values

Values are specific types of beliefs that are so important and central to one's belief system that they act as life guides. Values are central to a person's personality and are responsible for motivations and important decisions that have far-reaching implications.

Typically, a person will have hundreds of thousands of beliefs, a thousand or so attitudes, and around a dozen values. When it comes to money, many of us live under false beliefs that greatly affect our lives.

Money Training

Your money beliefs are a mirror that reflects the money attitudes
and beliefs of one or both of your parents and those of the seg-
ment of society in which you live. All of these have taught you a
lot about how you as a woman should behave with money—what
you should and should not do and what you can and cannot do.

Generally speaking, all money beliefs are a variation on one of
two themes: Money is evil; money is good. Whether we worship
money or hate it, when we hold it responsible for our happiness, we give it power. Whether consciously or subconsciously,
we choose the role money plays in our lives. So we—not our
money or lack of it—are solely responsible for our attitudes,
beliefs, actions, and happiness.

As a little girl, you were like a sponge. You soaked up beliefs.
You watched and listened. Maybe you absorbed fear, perhaps
adoration. You may have formed beliefs about being undeserv-
ing or incompetent. What you learned, starting with your first
moment on earth, has contributed to your adult attitudes and
beliefs about how to get what you want and need. All of these
beliefs have determined what you feel you deserve and whether
you think you are smart enough to manage money or believe
you must forever depend on someone else to get what you need.
The beliefs and therefore the attitudes you have about money
have a lot to do with why you always spend more money than
you have, why you don't believe you will ever get ahead, why you
feel so controlled by your finances, why you can't get enough
money, or why you don't believe you deserve anything.

I received a letter from a woman who told me of her struggle
with letting go of false money beliefs. As the oldest child of missionaries, she spent her early childhood and teenage years in a
foreign country. Somehow during those years she developed a
false belief that to serve God in a meaningful way you must live
in poverty. After all, why else would her family be so poor while

the carnal Christians back home in secular occupations lived in luxury? Her parents would often tell her that while they had little money and material possessions they were rich because they were serving the Lord.

Years passed and this woman became a wife and mother. She felt guilty for having nice things, for making more money in a month than her family had made in an entire year on the mission field. Once she was able to dig through her emotions and get to the heart of the matter, she discovered that her false beliefs regarding money were keeping her from enjoying all the blessings God had given her.

Once you accept the fact that perhaps some of the things you believe about money might be defective or downright false, you can begin the process of changing your money beliefs and thus your money behaviors. You will be able to let go of old beliefs that keep you stuck in either hating or worshiping money.

If you have been irresponsible or reckless with money, have allowed credit to control your life, have gotten into a tiny financial mess or one of behemoth proportions, or have failed to participate in the financial aspects of your home, it is not because there's something wrong with you. You are not fiscally defective! It's just that somewhere along the way you picked up false beliefs about money and the role it plays in your life.

Taking Responsibility

We are responsible for our own beliefs, feelings, and attitudes. We have to look to ourselves when it comes to doing something about our problems with money or lack of understanding about it. Blaming money, or the lack of it, for our problems and behaviors is no different than blaming others or God for our misery. We choose the role money plays in our lives, and taking responsibility for that is the first step in making necessary

or love!

changes. To take responsibility for our beliefs, we need to find out what they are.

Are you ready to examine your current beliefs and attitudes about money? Perhaps you're unsure what yours are. Frankly, I'd be a little surprised if you weren't.

Following are common beliefs and attitudes about money. Perhaps you'll find some of the attitudes in your own life, perhaps none. Regardless, learning about others' beliefs may help you figure out what your own attitudes are. Once you know what they are, you'll be able to examine them, identify those that are based in truth, and let go of false, destructive beliefs and attitudes.

Destructive and Self-Defeating Money Attitudes

Money as an Object of Worship

If someone had accused me of worshiping money, I would have said, "No way. I'm a Christian, and that's the last thing a Christian would ever do." I've since learned that is also a false belief because many people of all spiritual persuasions worship money.

By definition, worship is the adoration, homage, or veneration given to a deity. According to that definition, worshiping money sounds pretty sick, doesn't it? The person who worships money is convinced that money, and enough of it, holds the key to a perfect life. That person might also believe it is responsible for love, freedom, success, and joy.

Money worshipers believe that an increase in income or a windfall will make everything better. They crave the status they're convinced will come with the things that money can buy. They believe money will solve all of their problems. Sadly, I believe that this is the money belief pattern that afflicts the majority of Americans.

I spent years of my life worshiping money. Getting more and more of it became my central focus. I was in awe of what it was supposed to do in my life. Because my ego was insatiable, more money was never enough. I guaranteed myself a life of unhappiness because I was always waiting to be happy until I had enough money. I was obsessed with money. No wonder I was so miserable.

Money as a Mood Changer

Money can be as powerful a mood changer as the most potent tranquilizer—and as habit forming. Spending money, whether we have it or not, has become a socially acceptable practice—especially if we can justify the act because we've had a terrible week and deserve to buy a little something nice for ourselves.

When it comes to needing to snap out of it or get over it, spending money often does the trick. Yet it is a poor tranquilizer because the satisfaction of the purchase wears off quickly. It takes a bigger fix the next time to achieve the same level of mood change.

I spoke with a friend one day who through tears described how she is compelled to buy something for herself every day. If she doesn't, she feels so bad she can't stand it. Buying something somehow alleviates her bad feelings and gives her something to look forward to. She has been completely unable to give up this shopping ritual, even though she has become buried in secret debt and has closets full of new merchandise for which she has absolutely no use.

There's real danger in using money to alter our moods because it is very easy to become addicted to the act. We are easily addicted beings. Some people medicate themselves with a drug of choice, others with a compulsive behavior. For many women, shopping is an effective way to deal with fears and feelings of insignificance and loneliness. Their act of buying something pretty is like a mother handing over a pacifier to a fussy baby.

54

Money as a Measurement of Success

Do you relate poverty with evil and prosperity with good? Do you align poverty with failure and prosperity with success? That's what all our childhood fairy tales taught us, didn't they?

No wonder those who believe that wealth and success go hand in hand feel personal failure whenever they experience a lack of money. If you believe that your value depends on how much money you have, your status and self-image fluctuate along with your bank balance.

This false money belief can be very tempting because of the emphasis society places on the partnership between success and money. It's a rare person who does not immediately define success by using the word *money*.

What is success anyway? I don't know all the answers, but it seems to me that when we get really honest, true success is often far removed from dollar signs.

It is a freeing thing to separate the issue of money from your life's work. Once money is a nonissue, you will be free to concentrate on what really matters and what will last long after you're gone.

Money as a Means to Acquire Love and Approval

Do you feel driven to go on a spending spree, justifying it as benevolence? Do you tell yourself, "It's for the grandchildren," or "I'm buying for others"? Are you buying gifts, or are you attempting to buy approval and love? Are you being generous or purchasing obligation? Why is it that you always have to take the largest gift to the party or crave the feeling of status you get when you pick up the tab at a restaurant?

The person who is driven to use money to gain affection, approval, and love doesn't feel she deserves approval and love for being just who she is. She is driven to sweeten the pot with money and things.

Parents with this false money belief often overindulge their children with everything under the sun. They have the underlying goal of earning their children's love and approval.

Money as Evil; Poverty as Righteous

There is a money belief that goes like this: Money is evil, and those who have it are greedy, dishonest, sinister, and generally corrupt. If you have this belief, to be good you must be poor. Poverty is equated with goodness. There is an underlying fear that opening one's life to money is a clear invitation for evil to come in and take over. Hate and fear of money become the unspoken rationale for losing and mishandling money. I've known people who even refuse to accept it. They seem to possess an internal terror of losing their goodness to money.

There are women who have become addicted to poverty and have a very difficult time giving up the false belief that money is evil, as are those who have it. Those who hold this money belief equate their poverty with martyrdom and a high level of virtue. The woman with this belief feels more righteous than the money-grubbing individuals around her who are obsessed with materialism. Because of this belief, she is likely a compulsive under-earner, hesitant to accept payment for work she does. Her volunteerism is usually excessive, and she feels that her eternal rewards negate the necessity of fair payment here on earth. What money she does have she hoards, compulsively stashing it and then "righteously" living on a ridiculously low, poverty-level income.

Perhaps you grew up in a family with very low financial means. Your parents, in dealing with the situation, taught you the foolishness of money and the vanity that accompanies it—telling you that there are more important things in life than money. Money was a vice. Of course, these things are true in some ways, but the message you received was that if you are to be a woman of virtue you need to avoid money lest it corrupt your life. You didn't learn that money is the result of a job well done and that money can be used in a remarkable way to demonstrate your commitment to God's principles.

Money as Limited

Another destructive belief goes something like this: The money I have is all I'll ever have; when it's gone, it's gone.

As a kid, I remember feeling this way about colognes and other precious commodities. Because I feared that when these products were gone there would be no more, I never used them. I only looked at them. I still wonder what happened to those little navy-blue bottles of Evening in Paris.

This belief causes paralyzing fear of inflation, interest rates, cost of living, and the future. The most terrible thing about this belief is that it's self-fulfilling. Because we fear there will be no more money, we make sure that's exactly what happens. It's a lot like thinking, "I just know I can't do it"—and sure enough, you can't.

Women who believe money is scarce are often debilitated by the possibility of making mistakes. Because there's no room for error, there's no room to take risks.

Healthy Money Beliefs and Attitudes

Money Is a Tool

Money is a handy convenience. Without it we'd have to carry around chickens and pigs to trade for goods and services that we need.

We exchange money for our skills and abilities, so in a way it is a tangible representation of our life's energy. The money we receive as a result of putting our skills and abilities to use becomes one of life's most important and necessary tools. And a powerful tool it is!

Money Is Powerless

Money has no power of its own, in the same way your sewing machine or electric mixer has no inherent ability. (I'd be very interested in a lawn mower or a washing machine that had the ability to self-operate, wouldn't you?)

The truth is that no matter how fancy, how turbocharged, how modern or technically capable, any tool left in the closet or used contrary to the purpose for which it was intended is not going to produce the best results, and in some cases, the results can be negative.

The best example of this is the woman who intended to wax her car and picked up the power sander instead of the power buffer. They looked alike. Enough said.

Happiness and Contentment Are Not Based on Money

Each of us has a body, an ego, and a soul. Our egos are in search of happiness; our souls long for contentment.

Your ego is not a bad thing. It's that part of you that includes your personality—your thinking, feeling, and acting self. Your ego is responsible for your style and personal tastes. Your ego produces emotions and desires—and I mean all kinds of desires, from little ones to those that scream out to be satisfied. Some desires are for needs, others for wants.

Face it. Satisfying a desire produces happiness, and it usually takes money to fulfill desires. Anyone who says money can't buy happiness has never bought new carpeting or a new car or seen the look on a child's face on Christmas morning. The frustrating thing is that this kind of happiness always wears off.

Think back to a time when you longed for something. I mean really longed and yearned. You were nearly obsessed by your desire and could think of little else. Maybe it was your first car or a certain article of clothing or a new piece of furniture. When you finally got it, you were happy beyond belief. But the happiness wore off, didn't it? That's because desires once satisfied do not stay satisfied. Gratification received from fulfilled desires is, at best, temporary. That's how our minds and emotions work.

Your soul, your spiritual nature, seeks contentment—satisfaction with what you have, whatever your situation might be. Contentment is a learned behavior, an acquired skill. It doesn't just happen when you fall into the right set of circumstances. Contentment cannot be purchased, and that's the best news because it means contentment is available to everyone, no matter what their financial situation might be.

How to Change Your Money Behaviors

I discovered a secret, and I'm going to share it with you. If you want to change your money behavior, don't start with the behavior itself. I know that's what you've always tried to do in the past. Like trying another diet or another budget, however, attempting to manipulate the symptoms without taking notice of the belief behind the behavior will only result in failure. The behavior might change temporarily but not permanently. You must trace the behavior back to the beliefs that are responsible for that behavior.

One of the best ways to get in touch with feelings and beliefs is to write about them. I think you'll find journaling to be very helpful in identifying your money beliefs. The written word has a wonderful way of giving substance and form to nebulous thoughts. You can identify which, if any, of your beliefs are false, and you can write about the healthy beliefs, attitudes, and values you want to bring into your life.

With time and commitment to this project, you will acquire information and insight, and you'll be ready to form new and healthy lifelong habits.

5

Reforming Your Habits

Some people never realize that they can redirect their present incomes and become wealthy. They buy into the popular culture and ignore the wisdom of the ages. You are responsible for your choices. Recast your habits and you will change your life permanently. You may change temporarily by sheer force of will, but it will only be temporary. Habits, in the long run, will control your destiny.

John Hanson

Have you ever noticed how bad habits seem to come from nowhere, sneak in when you're not paying attention, and make themselves right at home? Mine remind me of weeds that push their way into a beautiful garden and arrogantly use their strength and amazing resistance to gain the upper hand. My good habits, on the other hand, are more like delicate sweet peas that require coaxing, cultivation, nurturing, and undaunted encouragement to build strong roots and grow into something of beauty. If only my good habits were as prolific as my bad ones.

Habits are those consistent, almost unconscious responses and behaviors that determine our effectiveness or ineffectiveness. A habit is a powerful force with the unique ability to be a best friend or a worst enemy. Our habits—how we behave day to day—are the outward and constant expressions of our character. What we habitually do reflects who we are.

Some of us act as though our habits were issued at birth and, good or bad, are as predetermined as our blood type and about as likely to change. Nothing could be further from the truth. It is possible to learn good habits and unlearn bad ones, no matter how ingrained or deep-seated they may be.

Habits are acts or practices we so frequently repeat that they become almost automatic. Almost automatic means that I, the owner and manager of my habits and behaviors, have not given up control to them like some mindless robot. I use them as a tool or a convenience, not unlike an automatic transmission, a bread-making machine, or a dishwasher.

I got into major financial trouble because I habitually repeated behaviors involving money, credit, and debt that produced enjoyable feelings and brought instant gratification. These activities were pleasurable because they blocked pain, masked fear, and fulfilled desire.

At first glance, that sounds like a pretty good method for coping, doesn't it? Don't kid yourself. Masking pain, anger, and fear by covering them with temporarily pleasurable feelings does nothing but make the masked emotions that much worse when the short-lived, pleasurable feelings wear off. And if that good feeling has had anything to do with credit cards and wild spending, a whole lot of guilt and anxiety gets mixed in.

The Power of a Habit

Habits can be learned and unlearned; bad habits can be broken and good ones established. Just think of the wonderful new behaviors we can unleash once we understand the power of a habit.

The secret to becoming a financially confident woman involves these three steps:

1. Investigate how financially confident women behave.
2. Eliminate habits based on false money beliefs.
3. Imitate and practice positive and beneficial behaviors so frequently that they become almost automatic.

Consciously identify the financial habits you desire to have in your life and then choose to repeat them frequently until they become almost automatic. That's the way to acquire good financial habits—or any kind of habit, for that matter.

Practically speaking, experts tell us that if we repeat a behavior twenty-one times in a row it will become a habit. Repeat it an additional twenty-one consecutive times and the likelihood is that it will become a lifelong behavior. That means it takes three weeks to establish a new habit if it is repeated on a daily basis and another three weeks to make sure we've got it.

It can't be that easy!

It does sound simple, doesn't it? If it were easy, we would have dumped our bad habits years ago, right? Well, perhaps. I'm the first to admit that just because I possess personal habits that happen to be bad and self-destructive doesn't mean I'm necessarily ready to get rid of them—easy or not. That's where the heartfelt desire to do the right thing comes in.

It's not like we haven't spent the better part of our lives making resolutions, promising to give this up or start doing that. Only a fool would opt to hang on to bad habits if replacing them with good ones was easy. It's not always easy. Neither is most anything else that results in lasting value and positive change. Yet, it's worth the effort.

There was a time I secretly feared I had some kind of serious disorder—or at the very least, I was hopelessly addicted to spending money. It did seem rather appealing to blame something or someone for my bizarre behavior. Being a victim, after all, is quite fashionable these days and did offer an alternative to owning my problems. However, I finally came to this startling conclusion about myself: I behave the way I do because of my habits. In the following chapters, you're going to read about nine specific habits of a financially confident woman. These habits are very personal to me because I previously possessed none of them. These are the behaviors that have completely changed my life. Here's how I learned the secret of reprogramming my habits.

The Twenty-One-Day Formula

I've told you just about everything else about myself, so here goes with the donuts. I love 'em. I've always loved donuts. They taste great. There's nothing like a high-fat, sugary donut to fill a nasty craving. Donuts are fairly cheap, very available, and quite fattening. It's the fattening part that really made me want to break my daily habit. I should have been equally driven by the fact that I was spending a fortune at around a dollar a day.

One day while listening to talk radio, I heard a behavioral psychologist talk about this twenty-one-day habit-forming theory. It sounded pretty easy, and of course I was willing to try anything my favorite psychologist recommended. My donut habit seemed like it would make an excellent proving ground. I decided that for twenty-one days straight I would not eat a donut. Bingo! I'd be forever delivered from a terrible habit.

It wasn't quite that easy. The third day was the worst. That's when it dawned on me I was giving up my beloved donuts forever—not for just three weeks. I was obsessed and could think of nothing else but donuts. If my memory serves correctly, I lasted about five days and picked right up on that donut habit like I hadn't missed a beat.

I didn't blame the radio shrink. It certainly wasn't his fault I was weak and undisciplined. I was just thankful I hadn't told anyone of my little experiment in trying to break a bad habit. I sure didn't want to fail out there where anyone could see me.

Quite a few years later, I recalled the twenty-one-day formula and decided I would use it to establish a new habit rather than break an old one. I thought this tactic would have a greater potential success rate since it's easier to do something than not do something.

My second attempt to experience the miracle of twenty-one involved wearing a seat belt (this was back before doing so was required by law in my state). I know, this is something we should just do automatically. And it's not that I would consciously choose not to put it on; it's just that I wouldn't think about it, and my car didn't have an annoying warning buzzer or light. This was a long time ago!

After about a dozen days, I noticed that my hand just went for the belt when I got in the car. After about three weeks, wearing my seat belt became a fairly automatic response. And after six weeks, I'd really made progress. It just didn't feel right not to wear it. I successfully created a new habit that continued for some time. Until we changed cars.

The new seat belt didn't feel the same. The start-up routine was different. Before I knew it, I repeated the not-belting act enough times (probably twenty-one) that the habit was unlearned. It was sometime later that I realized what had happened, and I had to go through the learning process all over again.

I learned one day the expensive way that the fine sandpaper of an emery board can permanently scratch the lenses of eyeglasses when the two come face-to-face in the bottom of a handbag. Just like that, my glasses were ruined. The cost nudged me to create a new habit. I designated separate pockets in my bag for these two items. I laid down the law that the two should always be put into their place and never the twain should meet!

I'll admit that at first it was more than annoying to stick to my pledge. I'm just not that fastidious by nature. But money speaks to me, and I kept remembering what it cost to replace those lenses. Day after day it got easier until finally I crossed the tipping point when the action became natural and then, in a short time, an automatic response.

There are activities in your life that you've repeated so often that they've become nearly automatic. Take brushing your teeth, for example. You do it so frequently and have for so many years that it is almost as automatic as breathing. And if we could capture this lovely behavior on video, I'm willing to bet you do it in the exact same way every time.

You pick up the brush with the same hand, open the toothpaste in precisely the same manner, start at the same place, and finish exactly the way you've done it since those pearly whites poked their way into your mouth. It's a habit.

Make a List

Make a list of the habits you would like to establish. Don't go nuts with pages and pages of entries because that will only discourage you. It's hard to imagine I could live long enough to establish all the habits I could write down. Think of the behaviors that are most important to you right now.

Perhaps one has to do with your checking account monthly statement. If you are not in the habit of balancing your checkbook every month, this would be a good time to make a personal commitment to break the habit of ignoring the monthly statement. (Don't worry if you don't know how to reconcile the bank statement with your checkbook register. That's coming a few chapters from now.)

In the case of a monthly activity, it will still take twenty-one consecutive repetitions to establish a habit. But that's twenty-one months, you shriek. So? It's a worthy habit to get into, and I know you can do it.

Becoming accountable to another person is a powerful way to make a personal change. I don't mean that you need to shout your commitment from the rooftops or publish it in the paper. Find someone you can trust to support you and stand by you in your desire to change. Your friend or buddy is not going to participate in changing you. That will never work. Yet, for some reason, the simple act of telling another person brings a personal commitment to a more conscious level. It becomes more important.

Tell that person you're setting out to consciously break a bad behavior by not doing it repeatedly until the practice is no longer almost automatic. Or tell your friend that you want to pick up a new behavior, and you will be repeating it until it becomes almost automatic.

You might want to think about enlisting the help of a child in your quest to break a bad habit or develop a good habit. Let me assure you that if you tell a young child you want help in refraining from donuts you not only will create for yourself a great reminder but also will think long and hard before trying to sneak a donut when the little fellow's not looking.

Plot the Calendar

As you think of breaking a bad habit or establishing a good one, twenty-one days, twenty-one weeks, or twenty-one months might seem like a long time. But remember your last birthday? And when is your next? Time really flies, doesn't it? Those twenty-one weeks or months (or years) will go by quickly.

They're going to go by just as quickly whether you begin to establish new behaviors or not. So you've got nothing to lose but a bad habit and everything to gain, including a good one.

A calendar is a handy tool to help you visualize the birth of a habit. Mark on the calendar the starting date, the ending date, and the twenty-one points in between. As you begin moving through the twenty-one repetitions, mark them off in an act of celebration as you move toward success.

Check Your Focus

I want you to know that I will never suggest you do something that I'm not willing to do myself. I know that some of the behaviors having to do with money are going to be great challenges for many, and I am facing a great challenge in the area of establishing habits even as I write. Changing behaviors starts with changing beliefs.

The next step is to consciously change your focus. We move in the direction of our focus, whatever it is. In the matter of finances, you must consciously decide to focus on positive money behaviors. The woman who successfully loses weight and goes on to become a weight-loss lecturer or counselor is a perfect example of a person who stays focused.

When I began publishing the *Debt-Proof Living* newsletter, I had no idea the fringe benefits I would receive from focusing on personal finance. I began the newsletter, quite frankly, in order to raise enough additional income to finish paying off our debts. I'd been fairly successful in changing destructive money behaviors, knew which techniques for getting out of debt and cutting expenses had worked for us, and wanted to share this information with others.

As you can well imagine, my daily focus changed almost overnight. In starting my new business, my focus zeroed in on one topic: personal finance management. To produce the best publication possible, I channeled my energy into research and communication. Twenty-two years later, I realize that my personal progress has been significant because I've been constantly focused. Publishing *Debt-Proof Living* has done more for me than for any of its readers, I'm certain. Had I focused on other areas and only delved into financial matters on an occasional basis, I'm quite certain we would not have made the financial progress we've made. We're reaching goals we hadn't even considered setting.

A Work in Progress

It's been several years now since I made a decision to do something about my woefully out-of-shape condition. It's not that I am not in excellent health. In fact, just the opposite is true. I have the world's most efficient metabolism. I could be stranded in a desert for three, possibly four, years with nothing to eat and maintain my body weight. And with a little effort, I'm sure I could actually gain a pound or two. My metabolism knows how to shut down so quickly and efficiently that giving up any body fat is unlikely.

Exercise has never been something of which I'm particularly fond. In fact, I hate it, pure and simple. I've never been athletically inclined. With this in mind, even I was surprised when I joined a health club. I wasn't smart enough to join one where I would find others like myself sweatin' to the oldies. No, I joined the gym where Hercules and Miss Universe prepare for their next competitions.

It took about twenty-one sessions with Trainer Jose (TJ) before my sessions became something even closely resembling routine. The first habit I had to establish was remembering to show up.

I won't even try to convince you that it was easy. It was very, very, very difficult. Everyone around me at the gym seemed to come by this weight-lifting thing naturally. Their well-cut, perfectly toned bodies moved in perfect grace and rhythm. I struggled with the most elementary routines, not unlike a baby elephant trying to get its balance.

Sometime into my quest to fit in as a regular at the gym, TJ decided to switch my appointments to early in the morning. I don't think I've had the opportunity to tell you that I was not born a morning person. How much of a morning person am I not? If forced to an upright position before the hour of 7:00 a.m., I have a pounding headache, queasy stomach, puffy face, crabby disposition, and overall defeatist attitude. I feel very sad and can cry at will. Believe me, it's not a pretty picture.

Twenty-one may be the miracle number for other habits, but to think it could make me do mornings was unbelievable. TJ assured me the morning schedule would be temporary. Even so, I kicked and screamed, whined and complained. The only reason I considered giving it a try was that my sessions for the following month had been prepaid. As precious as my sleep is to me, I preferred losing it to losing my money.

I made it to my 6:30 a.m. appointment several times. But as a happy person? One with the ability to say even one civil word? Not on your life. Just ask TJ.

I was miserable and made everyone around me miserable. Working out in the morning became such an unpleasant and impossible expectation that I quit. I quit the gym and I quit TJ. Habits are all fine and good, but some things are just impossible.

I went two weeks with no workouts, and as God is my witness, the most incredible thing happened. I realized that going to the gym and working out under the strong (and I do mean strong) arm of TJ had become a habit. It just didn't feel right not to go. I missed it and began to feel miserable. I had this nagging sense that if I missed twenty-one times the misery would go away and I'd slip back into my old habits.

I rejoined the gym, and gradually, one morning at a time, over the course of years, I have completely changed into a morning person.

Should you ever see me walking down the street, think kindly. I will never have an athletic build, and I've just about decided that a thin one is not in my future either. But I can curl some amazing poundage and am getting the hang of lunges and squats. I'm not half bad on the treadmill, and my resting heartbeat is becoming a much more respectable number. I've come a long way toward reaching my goal of being as physically active as possible until the moment God decides it's time for me to go.

Oh, by the way, since my original donut experiment, I've reapplied the formula to the problem. It worked. And continues to work now many years later. Not only have I not eaten a donut since I cannot remember, but I also don't even think about them anymore. And when I do, like right now, I really have no desire to break my habit.

This technique can be used to establish new habits, such as balancing your checkbook, ceasing to use credit cards to create debt, establishing a daily skin-care regimen, making your bed, or walking the dog.

In the coming chapters, you are going to learn the minimum— the very least—you need to know in every area of personal finance. You are not going to believe the transformation that will take place in your life as you begin to apply this twenty-one-day habit-forming technique to each of these areas of money management.

PART 3

NINE HABITS OF A FINANCIALLY CONFIDENT WOMAN

6

A Financially Confident Woman Is a Giver

> To give is to trust. It is to acknowledge that God
> will provide, that God will protect. When you give
> to God you create an investment in your own spiri-
> tuality, your community, your family and your faith.
>
> Judith Briles

There are three kinds of women: those who take, those who give, and those who divide the world into categories. Seriously, I have no statistics to support my contention, but it seems to me that the takers outnumber the others by at least a million to one.

While a person's propensity to be a taker or a giver may be inborn like any other personality trait, our society has certainly validated the takers—and possibly converted many of the natural-born givers as well.

Take credit cards, for instance. My credit cards offered me entitlement—the right to possess goods and services up to, and often over, my allotted limit. In my mind, it seemed that the merchandise in stores was already mine, and I couldn't rest until I'd bought it and taken it home. The have-it-all-now mentality has created a generation of takers, people who demand rights to which they feel entitled. No wonder this world is so out of whack.

Why Give?

Learning to be a giver is probably the most important habit you can learn in your quest to become financially responsible. Being a generous person, one whose giving is so habitual that it is almost automatic, will bring balance not only to your finances but also to your life. Giving provides the firm foundation on which to build all the other habits you're going to erect.

I can't say I actually understand how giving works—how it is that in giving we receive. I don't understand how computers work either, but I've gotten into the habit of depending on the fact that they do. The work my computer so capably produces certainly makes me a believing non-understander. The same is true of giving. I don't understand it, but I believe in its power because the results have brought me indescribable joy and happiness.

There is something about the act of giving that cannot be explained in purely rational terms. I believe with all my heart that the act of giving invites God's supernatural intervention into our lives and finances. I don't know about you, but I believe that opening my life to that kind of power is too awesome to miss.

Let me make this one thing perfectly clear. We should not give so we can get. What could be more manipulative than giving ten bucks on Sunday because we desperately want a hundred on Friday? Giving is gratitude in action. Anything more than a no-strings-attached manner of giving is manipulation, pure and simple.

The very nature of grace is giving. God offers us grace not because we deserve it or could possibly earn it but simply because he loves us. Isn't it ironic that the credit card industry has picked up on this thing called grace? They offer what is known as a grace period. It's that time between a purchase and the time interest starts accruing. During those twenty-five days or so, grace is extended in the form of no interest due. Grace—it is a beautiful thing.

I give to God because I love him and because I am grateful beyond belief for all he has done for me every day of my life. Giving from a grateful heart and expecting nothing in return is a sweet offering to the one who owns everything I have anyway. It's the very least I can do. And as I give, I experience God's grace.

Do you have a secret little problem with greed? Give! Is it tough to make the money last as long as the month? Give! Are you fearful of the future afraid you will run out of resources, financial or otherwise? Give! Do you somehow feel your success and personal identity are tied to the balance in your checkbook? Give! When you are the neediest is when you should give the most.

How much should you give? You decide. Traditional thinking from ancient times until now says that 10 percent is a good number. I like that and feel it is a good goal to set. If you can't start with 10 percent, start with something.

Where should you give? Good question. You need to be a good steward of your gifts, so a bit of research on your part is highly recommended. It's a good idea to check up on charities before donating, so take a look at sites like CharityNavigator.org and GuideStar.org. Learn what the charities and nonprofit organizations are doing, how they do it, and who is in charge. Personally, I am suspicious of any organization that is not open about financial affairs and whose overhead and administrative costs exceed 25 percent. In other words, at least seventy-five cents of every dollar I give should make it to the cause to which I've donated.

If you've never been one to habitually give, get ready to experience a whole new dimension in your life. I don't know of anything that will take your eyes off your own situation faster than giving to others. I am so excited for you because I know what will happen in your life when you learn the habit of generosity. If you want your life to have purpose, your finances to come into balance, and your faith to increase, become a giver!

I strongly suggest you add this to your personal belief system: Part of everything I have is mine to give away. Giving is an expression of my gratitude, a drain for my greed, and the way I keep my life in balance. If you really believe that, your attitudes will begin to reflect it, your behavior will change, and your life will be greatly enriched.

You may be tempted to brush this belief aside, thinking that in order to give you must have an independent source of money. Every woman, whether single, married, or divorced, has some money that comes into her life, something over which she has control. It may not be a lot and it may arrive sporadically, but the principle still applies.

Quick Tips for Giving

Even though giving is best done in secret, share with one other person, such as your spouse, a friend, or a mature child, your commitment to give.

Make giving your first bill. Make payment coupons and place them in the front of your bills-to-be-paid file. Or add giving to the bills you have set up in auto bill pay.

Give away a percentage of your second most-treasured commodity: your time. Volunteer at a local shelter, food kitchen, hospital, or church. Visit several such organizations and ask God to direct you to the place your talents can best be utilized.

Be a responsible steward. Learn about the organization or individual who will be the recipient of your charitable contributions. Ask how much of each dollar donated actually goes to the use for which it was received.

If giving doesn't immediately produce a burst of joy, don't worry and don't stop. Remember, it's easier to act your way into a feeling than to feel your way into an action. If you wait for the feeling before you start being a giver, you may wait forever. Ask God to make you a cheerful giver. The joy will come, I promise.

Each day look for little ways you can be a giver, even if it's simply holding the door for another person or assisting someone with his or her struggles. Once you catch this whole attitude of giving, confrontations on the freeway cease to be confrontational, irritating salesclerks don't seem so obnoxious anymore, and daily chores like laundry and carpooling take on a different meaning.

I am so proud of you for the decision you've made to invite God's supernatural intervention into your life. God will honor his promises! Your step of faith will be rewarded. Just keep expressing your faith in this manner and giving will become a lifelong habit.

7

A Financially Confident Woman Is a Saver

Saving money in the era of credit cards has come to seem quaint at best, a sucker's game at worst. We are taught that debt equals freedom but that's the kind of doublespeak in George Orwell's dystopic novel *1984*, where they claimed that "hate is love" and "war is peace." Okay, let's fix this mental glitch. Repeat after me. To have savings is to be free.

Vicki Robin

Friends invited us for dinner one winter night, which where I live in California means you might want to grab a sweater. The time of year and warm friendship blended perfectly with a dinner of homemade soup and honest-to-goodness homemade bread. I can say, without any doubt, that it was the most delicious bread I'd ever eaten. I had to have the recipe.

I soon learned I would need more than the recipe—I would need "starter." The instructions were clear. You must feed the starter every three to five days, at which time you must also take out one cup of this weird-looking stuff to make bread.

It was fun at first, making homemade bread every three to five days. But in a few weeks, I became distracted and busy. I found the time to feed my starter but no time to make the bread. So I split and fed and ended up with two starters in the refrigerator. And then in five days I had to feed both of them, remove one cup of the concoction from each starter, and either make two batches of bread or do the split action again. My family of starters quickly began to take over the refrigerator.

Soon I became nearly obsessed with finding enough bowls and loaf pans to get all this bread baked because I didn't want to waste any of the precious starter. Think Lucy and Ethel in the chocolate factory. Makes you laugh, doesn't it?

We had a lot of bread those first few weeks. But it wasn't long before it completely slipped my mind to feed my brood of hungry starters. You've probably already guessed the outcome.

I killed 'em.

Friendship Bread is a wonderful idea. The way it's supposed to work is this: You occasionally give a loaf of bread to a friend along with a supply of starter (there's plenty to go around, believe me) and the recipe, and that act of friendship starts the whole process of feeding, growing, baking, feeding, growing, baking in someone else's kitchen.

I calculate that about six months of this process, if followed impeccably, could fill every refrigerator in the Northern Hemisphere with jars of gooey stuff with the unique ability to make one feel guilty for not baking bread every three to five days.

It is a lovely plan, provided you follow it. You have to give away the right amount, you have to feed it, and you have to make sure you never use it all. You must always leave some in the refrigerator to grow for the future.

Which leads me (you knew I'd get there sooner or later) to saving money. Both money and Friendship Bread require a delicate balancing act. You must use some of it, you must give some away, and you must keep some to grow for the future. When it comes to finances, here's the bottom line: You can't keep it all, but you shouldn't use it all either. The key is balance.

While giving should be a priority in your money management plan, saving should be too. Think of it this way: 10 percent is yours to keep—not to save for a new sofa (saving is an excellent tactic for purchasing a new sofa, by the way), not to spend on next summer's vacation, but to keep. Yours to plant for the future. Yours to nourish and develop so that it will begin multiplying and working for you.

I have to tell you that it makes me excited to know what's going to happen in your life once you're convinced that a savings program is something you must have. And personal confidence? You'll gain more than you could have ever imagined.

Fringe Benefits

Saving money is its own reward. However, it has additional fringe benefits. Saving money is probably the best antidote for overspending. Saving money quiets the I-have-to-have-everything-now monster that runs so many of us ragged. It settles our spirits because knowing we've done the financially responsible thing by not spending all of our resources has a calming, quieting effect.

Saving money will bolster your attitude and give you the strength and courage to face the temporary sacrifices that may be required to get your money life straightened out. You see, once you have put aside some money, even if it's a fairly small amount, cutting back on groceries or temporarily giving up your weekly nail appointment becomes a choice you make rather than a cruel mandate over which you have no control.

Three years before we were able to rid ourselves of leased cars, we discovered that my leased car with two years remaining on the contract was worth about the amount of the remaining lease. The idea of selling it, paying off the lease, and sharing one car between the two of us made economic sense. But the thought of doing so was pretty tough for me to swallow. I'd had my own car since my early twenties, and I enjoyed the independence it gave me. I was nervous about giving that up and worried it would feel like failure, like we were losing ground rather than making financial progress. Owning status symbols and impressing outsiders are not easy to give up.

We kept talking about it, writing down the numbers, and projecting how such a move would bring us that much closer to being debt-free. Carpooling to the office we share would present no problem. But what about my speaking schedule? One car would never do on those occasions when we needed to go in opposite directions.

We made the decision to sell the car, determined to try the one-car arrangement for a while. If it didn't work, we'd deal with it when the time came. In the meantime, we agreed I would rent a car when I had a local speaking engagement.

That plan has worked very well for us. It's kind of nice to be chauffeured to work each morning, and I like driving a variety of brand-new cars when the need arises for a rental.

The best thing about the decision to go with one car after twenty-three years of having two between us was that we had a choice. By the time we made this car decision, we'd begun a regular saving and investing program. We were regularly putting away money that was growing for our future. We could have cashed something in or depleted an account to pay cash for a second car. But knowing we had choices made us willing to consider the most severe of the options.

I know myself. If we'd had no money in the bank, giving up my car would have felt horrible, not like the choice that it was. It would have screamed "financial failure!" in my ears, and I'm afraid I would have done anything not to give up that car—including incurring new debt. I would have looked at the situation as a husband-imposed repossession, and you know where that would have led—straight to resentment and disharmony.

Compounding Interest

You've already gathered that accounting and finance were never on my list of career considerations. Let me put that another way: Math gives me a rash. Remember, I barely got out of beginning bookkeeping. I'll never know why I actually selected that class let alone stuck with it. I don't like to think about numbers, formulas, axioms, postulates, or anything even remotely related. Believe me, no one was happier than I with the invention of the calculator. Yet in spite of my aversion to math, I find the matter of compounding interest to be fun if not fascinating.

Albert Einstein has been credited with saying that the magic of compounding interest is the eighth wonder of the world. That's how amazing it is. And then there's Alvin Danenberg, another really smart guy who's also pretty wild about compounding interest. Al, a practicing periodontist and a registered investment advisor, wrote a wonderful little book in language I not only understand but also thoroughly enjoy (*21½ Easy Steps to Financial Security*). Danenberg explains compounding interest this way:

> In 1492 Christopher Columbus decided he was going to save for retirement. He had one penny ($0.01), and he knew he could earn 6 percent every year on his money. He put the penny in his left pocket and placed the interest ($0.01 x 6% = $0.0006) into his right pocket for safekeeping. He never added anything to his

original penny in his left pocket. Yet, the interest accumulated year after year in his right pocket.

Chris is a very healthy guy: He lives until today—522 years later as I write—and decides to retire. So he takes his one penny from his left pocket and adds it to the simple interest in his right pocket. Do you know how much Mr. Columbus has?

Well, the interest in his right pocket added up to only $0.31 (522 years x $0.0006 = $0.31). Along with his original penny from his left pocket, he has $0.32 on which to retire. Not very good planning![1]

What could Chris have done differently? Let's assume Chris was much more astute about investing because he knew about compounding. Instead of putting the interest in his right pocket, he put it in his left pocket with the original penny—the principal. Over the years, he would earn the same 6 percent interest on both the original penny and the accumulated interest in his left pocket.

As the story goes, at the end of year one, he had $0.0106 in his left pocket (the original penny plus the 6 percent interest). At the end of year two, he had $0.011236 ($0.0106 plus 6 percent interest). At the end of year three, he had $0.01191 ($0.011236 plus 6 percent interest). This is called compounding and continued for Chris for 522 years. How much would good ol' Chris have finally accumulated for retirement?

The answer is somewhat more to Chris's liking. After 522 years of compounding the original penny at 6 percent interest, Chris has $370,007,768,814.68[2] (that's 370 billion, 7 million, 768 thousand, 814 dollars, and 68 cents). That's a lot of pocket change!

None of us will live that long, but all of us will have more than one penny to invest, and eventually higher rates of interest will return.

When it comes to interest, compounding simply means earning interest on the principal and leaving that interest in the account to become part of the principal so that it starts earning interest too. That's the "magic" of compounding interest. It's not really magic; it just seems like it.

As the economy in the United States continues to reel following the financial market's crash of 2007–2008 and the recession that followed, interest rates on savings accounts are still at nearly nonexistent levels. While rates of 5 or 6 percent were readily available in years prior, at this writing, it's difficult to find even one-half (0.50) percent. This doesn't eliminate compounding interest, but it keeps it very low.

This situation has put many people in a bind—particularly seniors in their retirement years who need their savings to be safe in a bank or credit union but also earning a respectable rate of interest.

Will interest rates on savings accounts increase anytime soon? No one knows, but I choose to be confident that eventually they will.

Another Story

Meet my fictional friends, Jennifer and Emily. They're both the same age, and they are committed to saving $50 a month, which is $600 a year.

Jennifer is smart and starts saving at age twenty-one. She saves $600 a year for eight years ($600 x 8 years = $4,800) and then stops adding more, allowing her money to compound.

Emily, who is a procrastinator, doesn't begin saving $600 a year until she's twenty-nine. But once she gets started, she adds $600 a year until she retires at age sixty-five. Emily contributes to her savings account a total of $22,200 ($600 x 37 years = $22,200) but cannot come close to catching up with Jennifer. The only difference in the way they saved? Jennifer started early.

Look at the chart to see the magic of compounding interest. Pretty amazing, isn't it? I tell you, this matter of compounding interest never ceases to amaze me. Now let me amaze you a bit more. Let's say that Jennifer didn't stop her monthly $50 deposits at the end of eight years but instead kept them up right to the day she retired at age sixty-five. Her actual out-of-pocket contributions would be $27,000, but her account would have more than a half million dollars in it.

This story has a strong and powerful message: Start early and feed your savings account regularly. Save as much as you can as soon as you can. The longer your money has to grow, the harder it will work for you and the more productive it will become. In our example, Jennifer contributed only $50 a month for eight years. Emily, who snoozed for those first eight years, had to contribute more than four times as much principal as Jennifer, and she still ended up behind at retirement by nearly $40,000.

Compounding Interest

Age	Jennifer Saves	Total with Compounded Interest	Emily Saves	Total with Compounded Interest
21	$600	$600	0	
22	600	1,386	0	
23	600	2,185	0	
24	600	3,063	0	
25	600	4,029	0	
26	600	5,092	0	
27	600	6,262	0	
28	600	7,548	0	
29	0	8,303	$600	$600
30	0	9,133	600	1,386
31	0	10,046	600	2,185
32	0	11,051	600	3,063
33	0	12,156	600	4,029
34	0	13,372	600	5,092
35	0	14,709	600	6,262
36	0	16,179	600	7,548

Age	Jennifer Saves	Total with Compounded Interest	Emily Saves	Total with Compounded Interest
37	0	17,798	600	8,962
38	0	19,578	600	10,519
39	0	21,535	600	12,231
40	0	23,689	600	14,114
41	0	26,057	600	16,185
42	0	28,663	600	18,464
43	0	31,529	600	20,970
44	0	34,683	600	23,727
45	0	38,151	600	26,760
46	0	41,964	600	30,096
47	0	46,160	600	33,765
48	0	50,777	600	37,802
49	0	55,854	600	42,242
50	0	61,440	600	47,126
51	0	67,584	600	52,499
52	0	74,342	600	58,409
53	0	81,776	600	64,910
54	0	89,954	600	72,061
55	0	98,950	600	79,927
56	0	108,845	600	88,580
57	0	119,729	600	98,098
58	0	131,702	600	108,568
59	0	144,872	600	120,085
60	0	159,360	600	132,745
61	0	175,296	600	146,689
62	0	192,825	600	162,018
63	0	212,108	600	178,880
64	0	233,319	600	197,428
65	0	256,650	600	217,830
Total	$4,800	$256,650	$22,200	$217,830

Figures are based on 10 percent interest compounded annually. You will not find this rate in a savings account currently; however, this is not unreasonable for money invested in mutual funds or other similar investments.

89

Make a Plan

How do you start saving? First, you have to plan ahead. If saving a specific amount of money at a specific time each month or week is something you don't presently do, you have to learn to treat your savings commitment as you do your mortgage payment and phone bill. As long as you see saving as optional, your chances for success will be so-so at best.

Let's say you decide to save $100 a month. To determine how much you need to save from each paycheck or other source of income, start with the annual amount (in our case, it would be $100 x 12 = $1,200) and then divide by the number of times you are paid during a year. If you're paid monthly, the answer is twelve times; weekly, fifty-two times; biweekly (every other week), twenty-six times; semimonthly (twice a month), twenty-four times. Here's an example of how much you would have to save from each paycheck in order to have a $100-a-month savings plan.

If you are paid monthly: $100 from each paycheck

If you are paid weekly: $23 from each paycheck

If you are paid biweekly: $46 from each paycheck

If you are paid semimonthly: $50 from each paycheck

There's nothing magic about $100. It's simply a suggested place to start. If you can't handle $100 a month to begin with, save less, but start somewhere. I suggest you make the amount just slightly more than what you feel comfortable with. I want you to feel the same way you feel when you work out.

Saving 10 percent of your income is the goal you're going to shoot for, and the closer you can come to that amount in the beginning, the sooner you'll reach it. The plan is for you to start saving and then increase the amount you save regularly until it reaches 10 percent.

Let me point out that the savings we are talking about here is from your net take-home pay or household income. If you contribute to a retirement account like a 401(k) or 403(b), this savings is in addition to that amount. Here's why. You must have an emergency account, what I call a contingency fund (more on this in chap. 11). If you are contributing only to a retirement account and you need that money because you are laid off or have a medical emergency, it will be very difficult—and expensive—to get your hands on that money. So think of your 401(k), 403(b), IRA, or Roth IRA as money that is out of your reach for now. Your contingency fund is money set aside that you manage and control.

Make a commitment that whatever amount you select you will save that same amount at the same time every month and that you will not decrease it if at all possible. If you do go through a season when you need to pull back, determine right now that you will get back to full savings as quickly as possible.

Find a Parking Place

You need to find a safe place to "park" your savings—a place that will be convenient but not too convenient. However, let me make this really clear: Where you keep your savings is not nearly as important as growing a stash of money that you control. It is amazing how many adult Americans have absolutely no money in savings. If that describes you, don't be embarrassed. Just be determined to change your status as soon as possible.

Investment or financial professionals would undoubtedly define "safe" a little differently than I do. They would want your money safe from inflation and loss of interest. I want the same, but in addition, I want your savings to be safe from you.

I know that keeping my savings in my sock drawer is not safe because borrowing it back is too easy. By safe, I mean having your savings in a place that is physically distant and downright inconvenient. I can't tell you the number of letters I've received that have recounted the same scenario: I started a savings account, but this or that came up and I had to use it. I want to help you prevent the temptation to take your savings back a little at a time until there's nothing left.

Local Institutions

The first step to safety is to open an interest-bearing savings account at a bank or credit union. Most banks, even some credit unions, require a minimum deposit to open an account. It might be $50 or more. And some charge fees and have other conditions. You want an account with no fees, no minimums, and no conditions. They're out there; you just have to look. I suggest you start where you are most familiar—the place where you have your household bank account. Or go to that bank's website and read about the different kinds of accounts they offer.

These are typically the kinds of accounts you will find at your bank or credit union:

Passbook Savings
NOW Account
SuperNOW Account
Money Market Account
Certificates of Deposit (CDs)

Keep in mind what I mentioned about interest rates in these post-recessionary times. You are not going to find high rates of interest presently. But stick with it. Saving money can be its own reward. Just keep saving, and then as interest rates increase, you will be better for it.

Online Savings Accounts

Also known as an OSA, an online savings account is one that is managed and funded exclusively on the internet through an online bank. OSAs are often characterized by higher interest rates, which surpass those of traditional savings accounts in banks and credit unions that have walk-in branches. By eliminating paperwork and reducing overhead costs, online banks are able to pass the savings on to the customer.

Online savings accounts offer yields (the amount you will earn through interest) that currently compare favorably with stocks and bonds, the liquidity of a savings account (meaning the cash is available to you at any time without your having to sell a stock or other investment), and the convenience of making deposits and withdrawals online. Most of these high-yield accounts have no fees, no minimum balance, and no lock-up period. Account holders may link their OSAs to their existing bank accounts for easy transfer of funds between multiple accounts. Some also offer ATM cards so that customers can directly access the funds in their OSAs.

A great website, SavingsAccounts.com, keeps track of online savings banks so you can compare them.

Make It Easy to Follow Through

Once you've determined the amount, frequency, and destination of your savings, you have to do one more thing—perhaps the most important thing of all. You have to make a commitment. What good is a savings account and a good understanding of compounding interest if you don't follow through. Don't be like Emily and wait eight years to make consistent deposits.

Make your own payment coupons, including the due date and minimum amount to be paid. If you will be depositing through the mail, make a supply of stamped and addressed envelopes. Now is the time to create all the convenience you can think of. Keep these coupons and envelopes in the front of your bills-to-be-paid file. When you have everything all ready to go, you won't be as likely to forget who's second in line to get paid.

But by far the easiest way to save money is to have it automatically deposited into your savings account before you ever see it. Automatic savings can be set up with your employer or with your bank. You can direct your employer to deposit a certain amount of your paycheck into your savings account each pay period. Or you might instruct your bank to transfer a certain amount from your checking account into your savings account on a particular day of every month. The principle is that if you don't see the money, you won't miss it.

In a short period of time, you'll not only not miss the money but also often forget all about it. And when you get just a bit too comfortable with your savings contribution? It's probably time to increase the amount.

There is a reason for your savings. I will tell you about this in chapter 11 and also help you determine how much you need to accumulate in your savings account. For now, it is important that you see saving as the second most important thing you do with your money. Giving is the first.

Ways to Raise Cash for Your Stash

Not everyone has a regular source of income or control over the family income. If this is true for you, making savings coupons or authorizing automatic deposits may not be possible at this time. So are you off the hook? No way! There are many other ways you can start saving. Here are some ideas to get your creative juices flowing.

Save all your change. This is probably the most painless way to sock away money each year. At the checkout stand, if your bill comes to $4.12, don't break out the coins. Hand the clerk a $5 bill and you'll get $0.88 to deposit into your change jar. When it gets full, simply wrap the coins and make a savings deposit. My husband, Harold, taught me this trick. He can't stand to carry around change and has a change receptacle in the car, another in his desk, and still another on his bureau. His all-time best change year netted him $1,100, and those were after-tax dollars.

Keep a bank in the laundry room. The way I see it, she who does the laundry keeps the cash. How do those coins and bills make it through the wash and dry cycle anyway? Unless your family is highly neglectful, your total take won't be much, but every little bit counts. I find at least $25 a year in the laundry.

Give up expensive habits. If you spend just $5 a day eating breakfast or lunch out, you're spending $1,270 a year, and that's allowing for two weeks of vacation. Eating at home or carrying your lunch two days a week will allow you to save at least $500 in the next twelve months. Imagine what you could save if you quit smoking, gave up lottery tickets, or cut back on other expensive habits you support.

Save all refunds and coupon savings. Instead of spending rebates and refund checks, save them. The next time you grocery shop, ask the clerk to give you the subtotal before coupons are deducted. Pay that amount and then ask for your coupon savings to be given to you in cash. Stash the cash in a special place or savings account, and you really will be saving money by using grocery coupons.

Hang on to windfalls. As you receive unexpected sums of money, such as gifts, bonuses, inheritances, retroactive pay, awards, and dividends, don't spend the cash—stash it. If you put those checks into your regular checking account, they will disappear into your everyday living expenses. Instead, deposit them—no matter how small—into your savings account.

Keep making payments. As you pay off a credit card or other loan, keep making the same payments, but instead of sending them to the lender, put them into your savings account.

Sell assets. It's a pretty sure bet that all of us have far more stuff than we really need or can possibly appreciate. Just think of everything you have to keep track of, protect, clean, store, insure, and worry about. What would you gain by unloading things that are robbing you of freedom? Sell! Liquidate! Give your savings program a jump start with the proceeds.

8

A Financially Confident Woman Is an Investor

The key to making money is to stay invested.

Suze Orman

You don't need to have an extraordinary income or spectacular education to become a successful investor. Take the story of one Ohio gentleman. Years ago, he, a typical blue-collar worker, became outraged by what seemed to be unreasonable utility rate increases. It's easy to understand how helpless he felt as he saw more and more of his paycheck going to keep lights burning in his modest home. It angered him when he thought of how rich those utility company owners were becoming off his meager wages.

As the story goes, our hardworking, middle-class fellow decided to show them a thing or two. Because his utility company allowed customers to own shares of stock in the company (most utility companies do), he decided that each month when he paid his electricity bill he would write out an additional check equal to one day's wages. With this second check he would purchase shares of ownership in the company. He figured if he couldn't beat them, he'd join them. As the years went by, he faithfully carried out his commitment, always making that second check equal to his current daily rate of pay.

I've been told that this man became the second largest stockholder in the company and a millionaire many times over. He was not a rich man when he began buying stock. On the contrary, by his peers' standards, he was probably on the low end of the spectrum. But he practiced the two cardinal principles of effective saving and investing: He invested a predetermined amount of money at a set time of the month, and he stuck with it. Little by little, his money went to work for him so that he was able to achieve financial security. Financial security is that point in time when you can live the lifestyle you have chosen financed by the assets you have accumulated without the need for any additional income.

There was a time in my life when I believed a person needed something in the neighborhood of two thousand dollars to start a real investment program. Of course, we never happened to have that amount of money just lying around, which was our excuse for not starting an investment program. I paid little attention to the fact that I didn't have a clue how to get started anyway. A lack of cash allowed me to remain in my state of investment ignorance.

But take it from me—one of the world's most mathematically challenged individuals, a woman who experiences total brain fade at the mere mention of investment terminology—you need not have a college degree or a lot of money to become an investor. What you do need is a sense of purpose, a healthy dose of determination, eyes that see beyond the moment, and a library card. The fact that you are a woman with the inborn abilities to nurture and protect makes you a natural at this investment game.

Saving is the simple process of amassing money. Other than earning small amounts of interest, saving is an inactive process. When you save, you don't expose money to risk. Of course, you don't expose it to reward either.

Investing is putting money to use by purchasing something offering profitable returns. Investing is an active and dynamic process. Investing implies a willingness to accept the prospect of risk in order to achieve even greater rewards. Investing is not synonymous with gambling or wild speculation. A wise investor always sees the safety of her investment dollars to be of the utmost importance.

Rules of Beginning Investing

There are three simple rules when beginning to invest:

1. Do not get into anything you do not understand.
2. Do not get into anything that is not immediately liquid (turned into cash easily).
3. Do not allow an outsider to control your investment or make investment decisions for you.

Years ago, I challenged myself to start a respectable investment portfolio with just $25. I'd heard somewhere this was possible. Frankly, it sounded about as likely as turning dryer lint into Persian rugs, but I decided to check it out anyway.

I shuffled through periodicals and investment books, and after nearly giving up on the idea, I came across a great book for beginning investors that gave me confidence I could accomplish my goal.

I decided that a no-load, growth mutual fund was the investment vehicle I would choose for my maiden voyage. I must confess I wasn't clear what all of that meant, but I felt confident enough to proceed. What did I have to lose? Twenty-five dollars is important, but I could drop that in five minutes at the grocery store without looking back or being concerned. Surely I could put the same $25 at risk in the world of investing without losing sleep.

What Is a Mutual Fund?

Picture this. You have a couple dollars, and you decide you want to buy stock, which, simply put, is a tiny piece of ownership in a large company. You call your local stockbroker and place your order for $50 of, let's say, Microsoft. You are laughed off the phone not only because the brokerage will not handle such a small transaction but also because $50 wouldn't even purchase two shares of Microsoft stock. By the time you'd paid the hefty brokerage fee (sales commission), you'd find this transaction to be completely unrealistic.

You decide to get together some of your friends (naturally, I'm one of them), acquaintances, and relatives and convince everyone to join you in your investment by putting $50 each into a common pot so that the group has enough to buy stock. There are ten of us, so now we have $500 to invest. We've created a mutual fund.

None of us knows exactly what to do next. Someone mentions a friend named Florence who might be willing to help us out. She knows about this kind of thing, and everyone agrees to appoint Flo to pick out some stock for us to purchase. We now have a fund manager. If we make a bad choice, we don't want to lose all our money. So instead of putting all our money into one company, we agree to purchase shares of several companies. Now we are diversified.

Flo, being a savvy businesswoman, says that she wants $25 for her trouble. If we agree and pay her the fee, we'll have $475 with which to buy stock. Our fund now has a load (commission to Flo) on the front end (before the stock is purchased). A murmur ripples through the group, and we decide to change Flo's compensation. No one likes this commission thing, so we decide to let Flo be part of the group and own a small part of the fund, but she won't have to put in cash. Now our mutual fund is no-load.

To keep everything straight, we decide to write down some rules for the group in case anyone has some extra money next month and wants to buy more ownership in our mutual fund or if someone needs their money back. This is our prospectus.

Flo makes excellent choices, and at the end of the first year, the stocks pay dividends (which are similar to interest) and go up in value. The group decides to instruct Flo to buy more stock with the dividends instead of divvying up the profit among us. Now we have growth.

Take the foregoing example; multiply the number of participants and contributions by several zillion; throw in heavy-duty laws and federal regulations; give Flo hefty academic degrees, some new clothes, and many years of investing experience, and we have a no-load, growth mutual fund. Simple as that.

Look, Learn, and Invest

Back to me and my $25 investment program. In March 1993, I made my initial purchase in an aggressive no-load, growth mutual fund (meaning this particular fund invests in riskier stocks). I selected this fund for a variety of reasons, not the least of which was I planned to invest regularly for the next twenty-five years. I would add at least the same amount of money at the same time every month without fail. I figured some months the price would be down when I bought and other months the price would be up. But overall, I believed it would average out to my benefit. This is called dollar cost averaging. I filled out the proper paperwork so that my monthly deposit was made directly from our checking account.

To be perfectly candid, I went months without even thinking about my investment, and that's the way it should be. Investments of this kind should be made for the long haul and not hovered over. The stock market has regular peaks and valleys, and watching it on a daily basis could drive someone like me over the edge.

In addition to this particular mutual fund, Harold and I now own many other investments. We research and make our decisions based on understanding. If we don't "get it," we don't invest. Not all of our investment dollars go into the riskier vehicles such as stocks and mutual funds. We've learned from the experts how important it is to have a strong, safe base for our investment portfolio (which simply means all our investments collectively), so we've also purchased savings bonds and other types of treasuries and bank certificates of deposit.

Please understand, I am not an investment counselor and certainly not qualified to recommend how you should invest your money. All I can do is encourage you to learn for yourself and then make wise and informed decisions. I promise that if you take the time and exert the effort to learn, you will be rewarded.

Four Characteristics of Successful Investors

Successful investors possess these four characteristics:

1. Successful investors have a plan, and they stick to it.
2. Successful investors invest regularly.
3. Successful investors are patient.
4. Successful investors do not "marry" their investments.

I have a good idea that once you get going you're going to love this new challenge called personal investing. You might even want to consider starting or joining an investment club. Here are a few other tips to follow:

- Never be ashamed to invest small amounts.
- Add to your investments on a regular basis to take advantage of dollar cost averaging.
- Don't hover. Watching your investments on a daily basis will drive you nuts. Just keep feeding them and let them grow.

9

A Financially Confident Woman Says No to Unsecured Debt

The interest you're paying on your past consumption
is just eating away at your financial future.

Liz Weston

I first encountered the word *debt* in 1959. The Lord's Prayer—and its reference to forgiving debt—was part of the Get-Your-Way-Paid-to-Summer-Camp-by-Memorizing-Thousands-of-Verses Contest. Anyone who could successfully rattle off every single verse on the long list was awarded the coveted week at camp. I didn't try to understand what debt meant; I just wanted a trip to camp.

I ran into a derivative of the word *debt* in my infamous high school bookkeeping class. Mr. Black attempted to teach us the difference between debits and credits.

The theory of debt again crossed my mind (briefly) when I applied for a $200 college loan. I belicve I have just dated myself. A loan with payments deferred until some more convenient time in a far-off decade seemed so benign, so manageable. With my future at least four times longer than my past, why on earth would I let debt become a concern at my tender age of eighteen?

By the time I hit thirtysomething, I'd experienced firsthand the phenomenon of being able to buy now and pay later, and, quite frankly, I'd found it to be neither easy nor something that brought satisfaction for any significant length of time. You might say I'd formed a love-hate relationship with consumer debt, and the love part was all but dead.

I allowed debt to creep into my life and wrap me in its tentacles. Believe me, it was trying its best to choke me to death. That's when I finally saw debt for what it truly is—a seemingly harmless little friend with a bent toward deceit and the unique ability to grow into an all-consuming monster.

Financially confident women do not feel prohibited from using credit, but I can assure you that they never think of debt as normal or commonplace. On the rare occasion they take on debt, it is well thought out and for a very short period of time, and they have a sure way to make full repayment.

True, credit has become quite commonplace, and there is no doubt it's here to stay. The problem is that far too many of us have become strangled in our own credit lines. Debt has a unique ability to destroy wealth, damage relationships, and dispel joy when it ceases being a tool and becomes a noose with which we hang ourselves.

Three Kinds of Debt

All debt falls into three categories: safe debt, toxic debt, and survival debt.

Safe Debt

Safe debts, also known as secured debts, are those that involve collateral. Collateral, or security, is something that has at least as much value as the amount of money you wish to borrow that you put up to guarantee your faithful performance. The best example of a secured debt is your home. Your mortgage is a safe debt because you have pledged to the lender that if you are unable to make the payments, the collateral (the house and land) becomes the lender's. Your car loan is collateralized by the car itself. If you don't make payments, the lender gets the car through repossession and you get to ride the bus. Safe debts typically involve a credit check to determine if you can afford the payment on the secured debt.

Both you and the lender have a way to get out of the loan if you want. If you decide you can't make the payments, you can sell the collateral to pay off the lender or just hand the collateral over to the lender and call it even. Safe debt gives you a way out. The lender can sell the loan to another lender if he decides he wants out. Secured debts come with the equivalent of a safety valve so you don't ruin your life.

Toxic Debt

Toxic debt is debt you take on with your signature alone without the requirement of collateral and without a wise professional evaluating if you can afford it. This kind of debt comes when you make purchases using a high-interest-rate credit card and opt to pay only the minimum monthly payment. Toxic debt is the result of spending sprees and frivolous decisions.

Survival Debt

You incur this kind of debt simply to survive from one day to the next. It is the result of paying for groceries and diapers with credit and allowing that balance to roll from month to month, gathering with it large amounts of high-rate interest.

Payday loans, gaining popularity in many states, have become one of the most common—and deadly—types of survival debt.

Meant to be a short-term loan, a payday loan seems harmless at first. Nothing will sink your financial ship faster than getting sucked into the payday loan cycle where you'll pay from 390 to 780 percent interest, and that's no typo.

Survival debt is the result of putting the rent on a credit card because your bonus didn't come through or because the rent money went to repair the car or pay the utility bills or buy clothes and diapers for the kids. It's toxic in your life and can wreak havoc in ways it's difficult to imagine unless you've been there and experienced the pain and the panic of this kind of debt.

In 2012, 40 percent of indebted households used credit cards to pay for basic living expenses such as rent or mortgage payments, groceries, utilities, or insurance because they did not have enough money in their checking or savings accounts.[1]

Safe debt is manageable. Toxic debt is reversible because you can stop being toxic. But survival debt? Once you start paying for day-to-day expenses with credit because you don't have the cash for food or shelter, you've crossed a serious threshold. Now you're caught in a vicious cycle.

You may believe you have no other choice but to keep adding to the gathering debt. But that's not true. You do have a choice. But you may need intervention to stop the out-of-control downward spiral.

Trying to manage survival debt is like trying to outrun an avalanche. You cannot run fast enough. You need to immediately get in touch with a reputable credit counseling agency that is a member of the National Federation for Credit Counseling. Certified counselors are professionals who are ready and able to help. They will work with you to tailor a confidential, customized program with solutions that work best for you.

Let me reiterate. You want to be sure you are dealing with a reputable and reliable organization (there are lots of look-alike credit counselors out there who are not legitimate; be sure you are dealing with a counseling organization that is accredited by the National Foundation for Credit Counseling). Call 1-800-388-2227 to find the office closest to you. Or visit NFCC.org to learn more about credit counseling. These are people you can trust to tell you the truth and to lead you out of the dark night of survival debt.

The Availability of Credit

Never before in the history of this country has credit been so available and debt so attractive. A bank credit card is available to most anyone who can show a steady source of income, which is just about anyone, including those on government assistance. While it is no longer lawful for credit card companies to send unsolicited credit cards through the mail, preapproved applications have become as common as any other type of junk mail. These applications can be as simple as a form requiring only a signature or as surreptitious as a large check made payable to the recipient that when cashed activates a new line of credit complete with transaction fees, hefty interest rates, annual fees, and an instant monthly payment.

Who hasn't stepped to the checkout at any number of retailers only to be offered an instant 10 percent off in exchange for filling out an application to receive that store's credit card? They make the offer so enticing, so simple, and so trouble-free.

With an estimated 181 million Americans in possession of more than 609.8 million credit cards with a purchasing power of $2.1 trillion on which they revolve $856.9 billion of credit card debt,[2] easy credit is more available than ever.

The emergence of new players in the credit card market means there's going to be more competition to retain you as a customer and to get you to sign up for new cards. You are a valuable commodity to credit card companies, but don't be too flattered. They have anything but your best interest in mind.

Debt Is Expensive

Would you intentionally take more than thirteen years to pay back a $3,000 loan at 17 percent interest if it meant that you would end up paying more than $2,650 in interest alone for the privilege? Probably not. But that's what happens when you choose to make low minimum monthly payments offered by the typical revolving credit card. And the ugly truth is that few people run up a balance of $3,000 and then stop incurring new debt during those thirteen long years it takes to pay it off, one pathetic minimum monthly payment at a time.

Don't think for a moment that the credit card companies accept such a small portion of the actual amount owed each month out of the goodness of their hearts or as an act of friendship. They're no fools. The amount you are required to pay as a minimum each month (from 2.5 to 4 percent of the outstanding balance) is actually the credit card company's profit—the interest you pay for the privilege of borrowing their money. If you pay off your entire balance each month, they've lost their golden-egg-laying goose. Ironically, cardholders who pay the entire balance in full and on time are known among industry insiders as "deadbeats" because they aren't paying their share of interest. That always makes me laugh when I think about it. Deadbeats!

The credit card companies make sure they get their money every month. By allowing you to roll the entire remaining balance over to the following month, they're pretty much assured you'll stick with them for a long, long time. Perma-debt is what they call it, and it's supporting a mega-billion-dollar industry in this country—an industry growing by leaps and bounds.

I don't know about you, but it's difficult for me to think in terms of billions of dollars. One of my Debt-Proof Living members sent in a bit of trivia that helped me understand the immensity of a billion or even a trillion dollars, which is how we now measure our national debt:

A dollar bill is about 0.0038 inch thick. A stack of one thousand bills is about 3¾ inches high. Ten thousand bills would be 1½ inches more than a yard high. A million would be 12.5 feet higher than a football field is long. A stack of a billion bills would be 59.2 miles high, and a trillion would be 59,186 miles high. Our national debt at $9.3 trillion would make a stack of one-dollar bills 550,430 miles high! The moon is 239,000 miles away, so our national debt in dollar bills is over 300,000 miles beyond the moon.

The same analogy can be used to visualize a person's personal debt. It takes $3,200 to make a one-foot stack of dollar bills.

But wait—there's more! Just like endless infomercials, our friendly credit card companies have something special to throw in, something designed to keep their finest customers loyal to the bitter end (and, yes, for many the end is very bitter). For those who struggle along month after month and manage to make their minimum credit card payments on time, an award is awaiting—a little something to brighten the spirits and lift the soul: a credit limit increase! And just as company executives hope, most cardholders look upon that letter announcing the increased amount of money available to them as a trophy suitable for framing, proof of a job well done. Credit card companies absolutely love those who play the game according to their rules.

But it's not only credit card debt that is expensive. Geraldine, a divorced mom of three teenagers, works full-time and has qualified for a $7,500 loan from her credit union. Getting this loan will allow her to take care of some house maintenance she's been putting off. It also will cover the cost of a much-deserved vacation (a cruise sponsored by a ministry she supports), and it will leave her with a little cash cushion in case of an emergency. She will be charged 16 percent interest over sixty months, and her monthly payment will be $182.39. Given her present financial situation, she concludes that even though it will be a stretch, she will be able to cover the payment on her present salary.

Unfortunately, Geraldine made no inquiries before signing the loan. The monthly payment was her only concern. But let's take a look at the full price tag—the real cost for Geraldine to borrow this money. In addition to repaying the initial $7,500, Geraldine will have to pay $3,443 in interest for a total repayment of $10,943. But that's not all. In order for Geraldine to come up with the $10,943 necessary to repay the loan, she will have to earn considerably more because she will pay the loan with after-tax dollars. You forgot about that, huh? So did Geraldine.

Let's say Geraldine is in the 15 percent federal tax bracket, must pay 7.65 percent in Social Security/Medicare taxes, and lives in a state with 7 percent state income tax. That's a total of 29.65 percent that will be taken right off the top of Geraldine's earnings. So in order to pay back the $10,943 in principal and interest, Geraldine will have to earn over $15,565 in gross income. That is Geraldine's full price tag for a $7,500 loan, more than twice the original loan amount. Amazing, isn't it?

A better alternative would be for Geraldine to discipline herself to make those same $182.39 payments each month but into the Bank of Geraldine. It will take her three years to save $7,500, but then it's hers to use for things she wants or needs with no debt hanging over her head.

Debt Is Dangerous

Debt is dangerous to your wealth, your marriage, your relationships, and your peace of mind. It's not so hot for your blood pressure either. Arguing about money is the top predictor of divorce.[3] I'm not saying that money troubles cause all divorces, but money issues get the conflicts going.

Over the years, I've received letters from people who are serving time for embezzling money from their employers. The stories are all so similar that it's spooky. Invariably, they go like this. The debts were so huge, the bill collectors so nasty, the family relationships so fragmented that I had to do something. I took only a small amount at first, but it was so easy. So I took a little more, and it just got out of control.

I received a letter from a husband and wife who are serving simultaneous sentences because they both became involved in breaking the law to deal with their debts.

Debt is not a pleasant thing. Unsecured debt, such as credit card bills, installment loans, and personal loans, is the worst kind. If you buy a house, which is a secured or safe debt, and it turns out to be more than you can handle, you have the option of selling the house, paying off the loan, and moving on to something else. Not so with unsecured debt. The very fact that the debt is unsecured means there is nothing of value being held to guarantee payment of the loan.

There was a time in my life when I regularly carried a very large and equally heavy handbag. So heavy was my bag that it turned out to be the cause of severe shoulder and neck problems. I've reformed in this area, and I now carry a tiny little thing just big enough for keys, lipstick, identification, and money. What a difference!

Carrying debt is a lot like carrying my heavy handbag. It is cumbersome and a constant burden. Taking on additional debt is like adding a shoulder bag, and then a backpack, and then another bag for the other shoulder. Just picture yourself struggling through life, carrying all this weight. It's difficult to get anywhere or make any progress, but the worst part is how difficult the journey is. Trying to stand upright with all this weight is nearly a full-time job. There's no time to look up to see beauty, to experience the joy of the journey. While others who are less encumbered pass you by, you can't help but envy their ability to take side trips and excursions. But can you? No way. You can't just dump the burdens in the trash or hope someone else will pick them up for you.

And when you pass through the struggles of life, such as sickness or unemployment, your debts don't magically disappear. They become heavier than ever. While it's hard to imagine, there are those (I know because I hear from and about them) whose debts become so unbearable that suicide appears to be the only way out.

Debt Destroys Options

Debt takes away the option to quit a job in order to return to school. Or leave a miserable job to take one that pays less but allows you to do something you truly love. Debt prevents us from following our dreams or following our heart's desire to serve others in some profound way.

I'm reminded of the young woman who felt God was calling her to teach in a missionary school abroad. However, her debts were so large that there was no way she could quit her present employment. She had no resources with which to pay the debts, and so she had to turn down the opportunity to go where she believed God was calling her.

Each time you increase your debt, you eliminate more options. The reverse is true too. Each time you reduce your debt or pay another one off, you get back more options, until the day you are debt-free and your options are at an all-time high. That's what I call freedom!

Get Out of the Debt Trap

If you are carrying heavy credit card and other unsecured debt, I have good news for you. You can get out. And I have a plan

114

for you called the Rapid Debt-Repayment Plan (RDRP). It is the easiest and most efficient way to pay off all of your unsecured debt. It is simple and logical and really throws a monkey wrench in the credit card company's plan that you should stay in debt forever.

This is the way out of the debt trap.

1. Stop incurring new debts. If you keep spending on credit, you will never be free of debt.
2. Get out all of your unsecured debts (credit cards, store charge cards, installment loans, and personal loans) and add up the current minimum payments. This is the amount you must commit to pay every month until you are debt-free.
3. Arrange your debts according to the number of months left to pay until they will be paid in full. Put the one with the shortest term at the top. This order is critical because you will get an emotional payoff as soon as you reach $0 on your first debt, and I want that to happen for you as soon as possible. Make your payments every month according to your customized plan.
4. When the first debt on your list reaches a $0 balance, add its payment to the next debt in line. Now you'll begin to see why I call this plan rapid. Repeat this process until you are debt-free.

One year from today, I guarantee that you will not be the same person you are today. You will be either better off or worse off. Get busy becoming debt-free, and you'll be so much better off.

10

A Financially Confident Woman Lives below Her Means

Living beneath your means is the only route to take to enjoy a secure and comfortable standard of living throughout your working and retirement years. Living beneath your means isn't a suggestion. It's an imperative. Spend less than you earn!

Jonathan D. Pond,
"1001 Ways to Cut Your Expenses"

Frugality. I was repulsed by the word until I understood it. Frugality is just doing whatever it takes to spend less than you earn. Another way to put it is "to live below your means."

What a novel concept.

Frugal doesn't mean tacky, frumpy, or stingy. It means we don't spend money we do not have yet.

The truth is that I am a cheapskate. Okay, don't panic. This is good, especially considering I used to be a credit card junkie.

In a nutshell, this is what happened. I made a commitment to stop spending money before we earned it. I stopped making calculated and arrogant presumptions concerning God's mercy. I stopped assuming he was going to bless us in the future with a paycheck, spending it now, and then hoping and praying he would pull through.

Contrary to the picture you may have in your mind, I don't live in a shack in the woods or forage for berries and grubs for dinner. But I do fix stuff instead of running out to buy new stuff. Another novel concept. I figure out how to use this for that when that costs more than this. We drive paid-for cars. We challenge everything and ask if there's a better way before spending money.

Frugality is not about pinching every penny until it screams. It's about making calculated choices that lead to freedom. It's about trying different things until you find what works for you and what allows you to live the best life you can without depending on credit. The payoff is that you don't have to worry about making ends meet or juggling the bills in the hope that you might be able to get them all paid before they start arriving again. It's about having the money to do and have the things that really matter to you.

Here's an example. I used to get my hair cut every four weeks. Then I figured out how to stretch that to six. That's four and a half fewer haircuts a year, which translates to, well, you do the math. Apply this kind of thinking to all areas of spending and just watch the dramatic results. Being a cheapskate is less embarrassing than you'd think. Unless you count that half haircut. Ha.

The Secret of Simplifying

Any woman with a lick of fashion sense knows that the secret of style is found in three little words: accessorize, accessorize, accessorize.

Men have it easy when it comes to accessories. All they have to worry about is a tie, a watch, a belt, and maybe a briefcase. Their shoes don't really count as accessories because they're almost always the same color and height.

But women? We have to deal with earrings, watches, bracelets, rings, necklaces, belts, broaches, scarves, glasses, stockings, socks, hair ties, headbands, handbags, briefcases, and shoes of every style, height, and color. Being properly accessorized is anything but cheap. Or easy.

First, it's a matter of finding suitable storage space. Now I've observed individuals who appear to be wearing every accessory they own, but we usually need lots of space to store all the accessories not currently in use. And that just screams for some type of time-consuming, fancy organizational system because, as they say, if you can't find it, why have it? Or as I used to say, if you can't find it, replace it.

However, in an amazing fit of sensibility several years ago when I discovered the loss of yet another earring, I made a rash decision. I would own one all-purpose, lovely pair of earrings. I would wear them all the time. Period. Why not? I wear the same ring day after day, year after year and have not yet been arrested for taking unacceptable fashion risks.

At the time, I didn't realize what a brilliant decision this was. This small change simplified my life immeasurably. I've saved all kinds of time not having to decide which earrings to wear. And even more time not having to locate two that make a reasonable match. Because I always knew the exact location of my one pair of earrings, I hung on to that single pair for many years. Eventually, one earring broke, which required a replacement. Then I received a pair as a gift, so I have two pairs now, but nothing like the amount of earwear I once managed.

Ironically, this idea, born out of a desire to stop spending so much money on earrings, has produced an even more desirable fringe benefit. Simplifying, even in the tiniest ways, makes my life more enjoyable. Simplifying helps reverse the process of being overpowered, overextended, overworked, and overcome by the pressures of life—pressures that are mostly self-imposed. Simplifying, even when done in a tiny way, has the ability to refresh the soul. You won't believe all the extra time and freedom you'll enjoy when you simplify, to say nothing of the positive effect on your bank account.

Living simply doesn't mean moving back to the land, ditching your favorite appliances, and slaughtering your own meat—unless of course that's your idea of simplicity. Simplifying means getting by with less while maintaining comfort, eliminating complexity whenever possible, and minimizing the time demands that have a way of devouring us.

Here are three examples of ways to simplify that won't impact your life negatively:

1. Stop buying clothes that need to be dry-cleaned. Maybe you prefer to spend $15 to $20 a week at the dry cleaners, but just consider the expensive waste it represents.
2. Make water your beverage of choice. Just think of all the cans, jars, and bottles you won't have to buy, lug home, and then lug back to the recycling center.
3. Sell stuff. If you've reached the point where you no longer believe the bumper sticker, "He who dies with the most toys wins," it's time to start unloading. Paring down is the cheapest, fastest, and most effective way to become financially sound and happy.

Spend Less to Save More

There's only one way to accumulate money. You must have more money coming in than going out. You have to make more money than you spend. You must spend less money than you make. This is a simple principle, and those who live according to it know the result: financial security. If you spend all your money, there will be nothing left over. And if you spend more than you earn, you're on the road to trouble with a capital *T*.

Affluent people are those who earn money and manage to hang on to a good deal of it by spending less than they make. Frugality is one thing that separates the affluent from the rest of us.

Perhaps the terms *frugality* and *thrift* cause you to grimace. I know that's how they affected me. The words meant nothing short of purchasing my entire wardrobe at a thrift store. No way was I ever going to buy my clothes at a thrift store, a promise I made to myself at age eleven. Guess that tells you where many of my clothes during childhood came from.

I plead with you to give up your biased ideas of what frugality means. Just give it a chance. I believe you may come to learn that being frugal and living with thrift in mind are actually virtuous characteristics. You need not fear becoming one big fashion disaster or less classy and dignified than you are right now. I have confidence in you.

When you think about it, there is little we actually need—that is, really need in order to sustain life. These needs of course are shelter, food, and clothing. These things are absolutely essential to sustain life. The next level of expenses are certain comforts we've come to enjoy and want in our lives. And finally there are luxuries, those things in which we indulge to pamper ourselves.

The ideal way to distribute our finances is this: 10 percent given away, 10 percent saved, 80 percent to live on—to cover essentials, comforts, and luxuries. Not easy if you've been used to living on 100 percent, or more, giving little (if any), and saving nothing.

Frugality simply means striving to get the very best value you can for each dollar and fully enjoying the things you have.

Frugality is not an activity reserved for the poor and underprivileged. Instead, it is a noble way of life that is to be admired. Frugality is the mark of a good steward, one who is pleasing to God. To approach life with a mind toward frugality is to celebrate life, to surround oneself with beauty, and to be content. Living a life of frugality offers a giant sigh of relief to those of us used to overconsuming and under-enjoying.

We are so wasteful of the abundance that comes into our lives and our homes. Right living means using things up, wearing them out, and even doing without now and again. To be frugal means to have a high joy-to-stuff ratio. It means balance—not having too much or too little but just the right amount.

Think of all the stuff in your life, a great deal of which you probably haven't used or even thought about in years. If it isn't truly useful or doesn't bring beauty and joy to your life, why have it? Think of all the things that take up your time and energy because they need to be dusted, polished, fueled, mowed, insured, secured, and fussed over. There's something refreshing about simplifying, about knowing when enough is good enough.

The key to reducing is to look at the whole picture. You probably do not need to eliminate one area entirely but rather to cut back a little bit in every area. Once you've kept a written spending record (chap. 12) for one or two months, you will have no problem seeing where the money goes. And you will know instinctively where the cuts need to be made.

As you look at your first full month of recorded spending, play with the figures a little bit. Muster all the courage you can and multiply some or all of them by twelve. It's good to see what you will spend on fast food, for example, if you continue spending at your current rate. Or the telephone bill. We fool ourselves by never thinking about total annual costs. Spending $60 a month for telephone service may not seem like much, but that's $720 in one year. If you reduce that bill by 30 percent (not difficult if you apply all the cost-cutting techniques available), you will realize a $240 savings in a one-year period. That's remarkable.

By now you've rethought your values, particularly those related to money. Focus on what you've determined is really important in your life and the lives of your family members. We get so caught up in our lifestyles that we fail to realize we're spending a great deal of money on things that don't even fit into our value systems.

Seventy-Seven Ways to Spend Less Money

Here are some tips for simplification that might work for you. Perhaps they'll help you think of other ways you can slow down and enjoy the things that really matter.

General

1. *Give up the myth*. Myth: Buying things on sale is a great way to save money. Truth: Buying things on sale is a way to spend less money, but it has absolutely nothing to do with saving money unless you stop at the bank on your way home from the mall and deposit the amount you didn't spend.

2. *Stop trying to impress other people*. If you can stop spending according to demands put on your life by others (through peer pressure or the necessity to keep up), you will see a tremendous difference in the way you spend.

3. *Stop shopping*. To me, shopping means strolling through the mall with nothing particular in mind, simply looking for great bargains and things that happen to strike my fancy. That is a very dangerous thing to do. I'm not suggesting that you never buy anything again but that your spending should be a planned act of acquiring the goods and services you need, not spur-of-the-moment, impulsive spending.

123

4. *Anticipate.* There's nothing more frustrating than waking up in the morning to water gushing from a water heater with a rusted-out bottom or a flat tire with the steel belts exposed. You have no choice but to replace these items immediately. Now, had you anticipated the tire was about shot or the age of the water heater meant you were on borrowed time, you could have watched for sales and had time to comparison shop. But now you've no choice but to get whatever you can by any means possible. And you will invariably spend a great deal more, especially if you have to make that purchase on credit.

5. *Purchase with cash.* Retailers are keenly aware of the statistics that you will spend at least 30 percent more if you are in a store with a credit card, debit card, or checkbook. The last thing they want is a customer who carries cash. Why? Because they know how cautious and nonimpulsive the cash buyer is.

6. *Keep a spending record.* Seeing where your money goes keeps you from lapsing into a spending coma.

7. *Save first, spend later.* Instead of putting large purchases on a credit card, save first. Once you have enough cash, make the purchase. Amazingly, by the time you save the money, you may have changed your mind a dozen times. You might even have decided you no longer need or want it.

8. *Combine errands.* Instead of running all over town several days a week, combine all your errands into one trip.

9. *Use baking soda.* It's cheap. And it cleans and shines chrome, unclogs drains, removes hard-water marks, cleans plastic, removes odors, degreases, removes stains from marble, cleans fiberglass, removes crayon stains from washable walls, and, when added (½ cup per load) to laundry with liquid detergent, greatly improves effectiveness.

10. *Use a budget.* BudgetSimple is a free and easy-to-use online budget that will help you figure out how to get your finances on track (available at BudgetSimple.com). BudgetSimple helps

you spend less than you make by prompting you to log your actual expenses against your plan.

Cars

11. *Reassess transportation.* Perhaps you don't really need more than one vehicle. Many cities have public transportation systems. Have you tried yours lately?

12. *Find the cheapest gas.* It takes only a few seconds to log on to GasBuddy.com to find the cheapest gas in your neighborhood the day you need to fill up.

13. *Do it yourself.* Take a course in basic auto repair to learn how to change your oil, oil filter, and antifreeze. Learn to spot a hose that needs to be replaced and detect the origin of a fluid leak.

14. *Buy, don't lease.* Generally speaking, leasing a new car is the most expensive way to go. It's better to purchase a late-model used car. The major depreciation of the car will have occurred during its first year when someone else owned it.

15. *Keep your tires filled.* Check them weekly to make sure they're properly inflated, holding exactly the amount of air pressure as recommended on the sidewall of the tire. You should be able to increase gas mileage by up to 10 percent.

16. *Keep your trunk empty.* The more weight you're hauling around, the fewer miles per gallon you'll get from your fuel. So unload all that heavy stuff you've been carrying around. For the best performance, limit your trunk's contents to the necessary safety emergency equipment recommended by the manufacturer in the owner's manual.

17. *Locate a reliable and trustworthy mechanic.* The best time to do this is before you need one. Get a recommendation from a friend, relative, or neighbor.

18. *Increase your automobile insurance deductible.* Chances are excellent that if you increase your deductible to around $500, you will receive a greatly reduced premium. Check with your agent.

Food

19. *Grocery shop with a list.* A list is your game plan. Entering the store without it is flirting with financial disaster. The food industry spends $6 billion a year to weaken your resistance with fancy packaging and compelling displays. Staying out of the store unless absolutely necessary will decrease your exposure time.

20. *Arrive at the grocery store with cash only.* You will become a much more careful consumer as a cash buyer. This is particularly helpful for the compulsive shopper who would rather stick toothpicks under her fingernails than go through the checkout only to find out she doesn't have enough money.

21. *Be brand flexible.* Staying loyal to a specific brand might be a noble endeavor, but it will cost you a lot of money in the long run. If you are willing to go with what's on sale and the brand for which you have a doubled coupon, you'll end up keeping more of your money.

22. *Shop solo.* Your concentration will be better if you leave the kids at home, and you'll get out of the store faster. And your kids won't fall into temptation purposely set by smart marketing organizations. On your next trip to the store, stoop down a bit and check out what's been strategically placed at the eye level of small shopping-cart passengers.

23. *Shop at the cheapest store.* Most cities have stores with prices that are consistently less. Shop there.

24. *Purchase spices from an ethnic food store.* Many ethnic markets offer spices in bulk, allowing you to purchase as little or as much as you need. Prices? Just a fraction of the prepackaged version.

25. *Think vegetarian.* Once or twice a week, prepare a meatless meal. Serve meat as a side dish or an ingredient rather than as the entrée.

26. *Make your own baby food.* Experts agree there is no superior nutritional benefit to store-bought baby food compared to

food made at home. It rates high only on convenience. Caution: Never substitute your own formula or rice cereal. These are the only exceptions. Use your blender to puree food, then place the food in ice-cube trays and freeze. Food cubes can be stored in zip-type plastic bags and thawed out as needed.

27. *Use sale ads.* Plan your meals and shopping list around what's on sale this week.

28. *Stock up on sale items.* If possible, buy enough of an item when it's on sale to last until the next time it hits the sale sheet.

29. *Use coupons.* Use them only for items you'd buy even if you didn't have the coupon. Always buy the smallest qualifying size when using a coupon. Join TheGroceryGame.com if you are really serious about using coupons to slash your grocery bill.

30. *Double coupons.* If you are a couponer, find a store that doubles their value.

31. *Double milk's useful life.* Simply add a pinch of salt to milk when it's first opened. This will retard bacteria growth but will not affect the taste.

32. *Investigate store brands.* Most grocery store chains have their own private labels. In most cases, the product is the same as a name brand (usually packaged in the same plant) and labeled under the store's name. The price is always less. National brands are priced higher because the costs of advertising must be added into the price of the product.

33. *Weigh produce.* Prepackaged produce must have a minimum weight as printed on the packaging. However, not all potatoes are created equal, so a ten-pound bag may weigh eleven pounds, and a one-pound bag of carrots may weigh more than exactly one pound.

34. *Know your prices.* Compile your own price book. List all the items you buy regularly, the regular prices from the stores in your area, and the per-unit price (per ounce, for example). Now you will know if a sale is really a sale. Retailers are smart.

They know if they put a display at the end of an aisle with a big sign announcing "special," consumers will assume they're getting a bargain. If you know your prices, you won't be fooled.

35. *Buy in bulk cautiously.* It's no bargain if you end up throwing some away because it spoiled before it could be consumed. Break down large quantities into smaller plastic bags that can be sealed or frozen for future use.

36. *Consider out of sight, out of mind.* This can work in your favor or against it. If you have a case of soda pop you picked up at a great price, hiding it under a bed might be a good way to keep the kids from drinking it all in one afternoon. On the other hand, a roast purchased on sale and slipped into the freezer could be forgotten for many months, during which time it might spoil. Enzymatic action is not arrested during the freezing period.

37. *Buy in season.* It takes a little research to know what's coming into season and what's not. Out-of-season produce is the most expensive. Stick to what's plentiful and therefore cheaper.

38. *Know that expired doesn't always mean bad.* Because of store policy, many foods that are still wholesome are reduced in price when approaching their expiration dates. Many products reduced for quick sale can be a wonderful bargain. Ask the butcher and produce manager what's about to expire. Offer to take it off their hands provided the price is right.

39. *Empty the pantry.* Most of us have pantries and freezers full of stuff we don't even consider using. By being creative and building menus around what you already have, you might be able to increase the time between grocery-shopping trips. Every day you don't go in the supermarket is another day you can't make an impulse purchase.

40. *Buy local produce.* Typically, your local farmer's market will have better prices for far better products. But make a list and stick to it. A beautiful produce market can be as deadly as

a beautiful mall. And produce spoils quickly. Buy only what you can reasonably consume.

41. *Avoid convenience food.* The closer you can stay to basic ingredients such as eggs, sugar, and flour (also known as cooking from scratch!), the less money you will spend.

42. *Substitute, experiment.* Many people worry about meticulously following a recipe, as if the slightest deviation could change their ambrosia to Alpo. Lighten up. If a recipe calls for a cup of bacon when you have leftover ham in the refrigerator, use the ham.

43. *Join a membership warehouse club.* Approach this tip with caution. Make sure you will save at least the amount of your membership fee. And get a grip on your impulsive nature or you could end up owning cases of stuff you really cannot use.

44. *Eat lunch . . . for dinner.* When eating out at dinnertime, ask to see the lunch menu or request the luncheon portion of the item you select. Typically, you will save 20 percent, with the added benefit of having a lighter meal.

Banking

45. *Don't bounce checks.* With banks currently charging around $30 per occurrence, bouncing a check can have quite a punitive result. And don't forget that the merchant who took your bad check may have a returned check charge that can be around $25 or more. Bouncing checks can be financially deadly.

46. *Find a free account.* It may take some searching, but many banks offer free accounts with a minimum balance.

47. *Ask for free checks.* Some banks give free checks (don't expect anything fancy) if you ask. If you can't manage free checks, at least buy your checks directly from a check printer like Checks Unlimited (1-800-210-0468; ChecksUnlimited.com) or Checks in the Mail (1-800-733-4443; ChecksInTheMail.com). You can save up to 60 percent of the price the bank charges.

48. *Consider a nonbank.* Credit unions are often better and cheaper alternatives for handling your money. Typically, credit unions are smaller, which allows for more personalized service. Credit unions are nonprofit organizations more interested in benefiting their membership than amassing big profits, which is reflected in lower interest rates and fees, and generally have higher standards when it comes to qualifying borrowers and loan-to-deposit ratios. You need to qualify to join a credit union. Check the Credit Union National Association website at CUNA .org to find a credit union you can join.

49. *Use online bill pay.* Paying your bills online through your bank's website or an independent bill-paying site will save you a lot of grief, time, and money. You won't have to pay postage, and you'll have an electronic record of your banking activity.

50. *Be wise about ATMs.* Use only automated teller machines (ATMs) that are connected to your bank's system and for which you will not be charged a transaction fee.

Utilities

51. *Find the water leaks.* Give your home this test. Turn off all running water in the house. Find your water meter and take a look. Is it still moving? Chances are you have a water leak, and chances are even better it's in your toilet. Put a few drops of food coloring into the toilet's tank. If without flushing the color shows up in the bowl, it's leaking! Pick up a simple kit at a home improvement store to fix it yourself.

52. *Fix leaky faucets.* A faucet leaking sixty drops a minute wastes 113 gallons of water a month. That's 1,356 gallons a year!

53. *Use cold water for laundry.* The bulk of your laundry is only lightly soiled. Modern-day detergents do just as well with cold water as with warm. Your colors will last longer too.

54. *Experiment.* You may be able to use as much as 50 percent less laundry detergent than recommended by the manufacturer, depending on the properties of your water.

55. *Install dimmers.* Anything you can do to reduce the number of watts you use will reduce your electricity bill.

56. *Select energy-efficient appliances.* Use the yellow energy guide labels to make your choices. These appliances consume less energy.

57. *Use slow and pressure cookers.* Electric burners, gas flames, and traditional ovens are far more expensive to operate than Crock-Pots and pressure cookers. Anything that radiates heat wastes energy.

58. *Plug money leaks.* Take advantage of your community's free or low-cost programs for insulating your home. Check with your utility companies or community action center.

59. *Turn on to efficiency.* Install a simple light switch timer in rooms you do not use all the time like the laundry room, basement, and so on. Now those lights will turn off automatically.

60. *Get out of hot water.* You'll save heat and water in the dishwasher if you wash only full loads and choose the air-dry option. Don't prerinse dishes. Lower the water heater temperature to 120° F and let the dishwasher do the rest.

61. *Create body heat.* Raise your body temperature one degree by wearing slacks instead of skirts. Light, long-sleeved sweaters add another two degrees of heat; heavy sweaters, four degrees; and two light sweaters, five degrees (due to the insulation layer of air between them). For extra warmth, put on heavy socks with your slippers. Add a quilt to your bed.

62. *Turn the thermostat down.* In the winter, keep thermostats set to sixty-five degrees by day and sixty degrees by night unless you are elderly, in poor health, or taking certain types of medication, in which case you should consult your physician.

63. *Plug air leaks.* Here's how to check for air leaks. Shut the doors and windows. Move a lighted candle around the

131

perimeters of the doors and windows. If the flame flickers, you have an air leak. Plug it with caulk and weather stripping.

64. *Install a programmable thermostat.* These are reasonably priced and will pay for themselves in no time at all in reduced heating/cooling bills.

65. *Turn them off.* Turn off electric stove burners and the oven several minutes before the specified cooking time. The retained heat will keep on cooking.

66. *Cook multiple dishes.* When using the oven, cook several dishes at the same time. Use a timer and don't open the door if at all possible until the cooking time is completed.

67. *Check the refrigerator seal.* If it's loose, replace it. Cold air is probably escaping, causing the motor to run more.

68. *Write postcards instead of calling.* Unless you need to hear a voice, a simple postcard can accomplish the same thing as a long-distance call. And it's cheap—only thirty-four cents as of this writing. Keep a stack of postcards by the phone to remind you.

69. *Use toll-free numbers.* Before calling a company's long-distance number, check the toll-free number directory at Inter800 .com to see if that company has an 800, 888, or other toll-free number.

Entertainment

70. *Make a switch.* Instead of going to dinner and a movie, go to a bargained-priced matinee and have dinner or dessert afterward.

71. *Have potlucks instead of dinner parties.* The ultimate no-obligation gathering where everyone brings a part of the meal is a great social occasion.

72. *Escape to the library.* You'll be amazed what fun you and your kids can have at the library. You can borrow DVDs, CDs, and books on tape in addition to fabulous books. Some libraries have story time and documentary film showings.

73. *Go for a walk.* Chances are you live in a neighborhood you've never explored up close and personally.

74. *Write a book of your family's history.* Let the kids write and illustrate their own personal chapters.

75. *Hold a neighborhood kids' art fair.* Display all the artwork and ask adults to purchase their favorites. Let children vote on which charity will receive the proceeds.

76. *Be a tourist in your own city.* Go online and search your community as if you were a tourist coming for a visit. You will be surprised what activities you will find, many of them free or highly discounted.

77. *Shop in heels.* I'm talking your highest stilettos, girlfriend! A study at Brigham Young University found that when we have to work at keeping our balance, there's some kind of crossover mind-set that results in our making frugal choices.[1]

11

A Financially Confident Woman Is Prepared for Emergencies

> The idea behind an emergency fund is to store at
> least six months of net income for the sake of "just
> in case." Just in case your job goes "poof." Just in
> case your car conks out.
>
> Alexa von Tobel

No matter your situation—even if you are up to your eyeballs in credit card debt—you must have an emergency fund. Every household needs one. It is as essential to your getting out of debt as water is to your health. Without it you won't go far.

A Contingency Fund

In chapter 7, you learned the second most important thing you must do with your money: save at least 10 percent in a savings account. Now let's give that account a name—contingency fund—and a savings goal: at least enough money to pay all of your bills without a paycheck for at least three months; six is better. Or, in the interest of simplicity, let's set your goal at $10,000.

First, face the facts regarding job and income security. Don't count on it. With technology increasing at a breakneck speed and the nation's economic system having more peaks and valleys than a roller coaster, it's almost certain that at some point your income will at least temporarily be cut off. It's going to happen, so plan on it instead of being blindsided by it.

Start with baby steps. I agree that a figure equal to six months' income is rather overwhelming—paralyzingly so. Instead of focusing on that big number, cut it up into bite-sized pieces. How much would it take for you to live one week without income? Let's just assume that number is $600. I'm not saying that amount would cover your house payment or rent, but $600 might be enough to keep gas in the car, food on the table, and the utilities paid.

Focus on saving enough money so that your contingency fund (CF) equals one week's living expenses. That is an achievable goal. Then move to two weeks, a month, and so on. In no time, if you keep your eye on the goal, you will achieve a fully funded contingency fund. And that is going to make all the difference in the world for you. Your sense of financial fear will disappear. You will find yourself less prone to overspend. Your financial confidence will soar!

It's Counterintuitive

I know this may be grating on your nerves—the idea that you should be saving money. I agree that when you're in debt and so anxious to get out of debt it doesn't make sense to keep money for yourself. Common sense says you should be sending your creditors every nickel you can scrape together.

It seems right perhaps, but it's not. That's the same "common sense" that says it's okay to use credit cards to buy stuff and pay for it later, the same "common sense" that says if you are severely overweight you should not eat again until you have achieved your goal weight. It's a nice thought, but it's just not going to happen. You'll be able to follow that kind of thinking only until you get hungry if we're talking weight or until something unexpected happens when talking about money and credit.

Benefits

Face it. Getting out of debt is no simple feat. It takes commitment, knowledge, and most of all endurance. You didn't get into this much debt overnight, so it's going to take longer than a few days to get out. This will not be a sprint but rather a marathon. Your contingency fund will be the assurance you need to see it to the finish line. Here are five benefits to creating a contingency fund:

1. *It is the antidote for your credit card habit.* Just knowing you have money in the bank quiets that thing inside of you that demands to have stuff right now, even when you have no money to pay for it.

2. *It counteracts the feeling of being broke.* One of the reasons you are in debt is that you can't stand feeling poor. No one likes being broke, but some of us like it a lot less than others. Curiously, a pocket of credit cards makes us feel rich in a really false way. Knowing you have money in the bank is the authentic way not to feel broke—even when you are determined not to touch the money you have stashed away.

3. *It gives you an alternative to hitting the panic button.* When you're broke, you live on the edge of panic. And when even the smallest thing happens, even if it is not a true emergency, it feels like one because you press the panic button. Having money in the bank allows you to calm down so you can think rationally.

4. *It's the lifesaver that keeps you afloat while going through deep waters.* If you can make it all the way from right now to paying off your last debt without facing some unexpected expense (tires, water heater, medical expense, car repair, and so on), you will be fortunate indeed. And you'll arrive with an intact CF.

   The chances are far greater, however, that while on your journey to becoming debt-free something unexpected will happen. It's your CF that will allow you to keep going without having to run back to your credit cards for a bailout. Just imagine how defeated you would feel should that happen. Of course, you could start over again, but you want to do everything possible to avoid getting off course.

5. *It's your guarantee that you'll make it to the finish line.* I say this on the basis of my own experience and that of countless readers who are now debt-free. Having a CF, whether fully funded or in process, is the secret to your debt-free success. It's that second wind we all depend on when we've come to the end of our endurance but there's still more journey ahead.

A contingency fund creates the margin you need to move away from the edge. Since my financial reformation, I have come to look upon this matter of an emergency fund as wise advice. More than that, I believe it is absolutely essential if financial peace is to be achieved, and I've learned it is possible to make this seeming impossibility become reality.

For some of us, "emergency" can mean anything from the midyear sale at Nordstrom to a 3:13 a.m. hospital trip. I used to operate much like the federal government. Once I declared a situation an emergency, I could override all limitations on spending.

Christmas became an emergency. Perhaps you've experienced it. It's December 15, the kids are entitled to a great Christmas, which is measured, of course, by the number and size of gifts. We have no money. We call the credit card companies to plead for credit-line increases. Given the increases, we now feel authorized to run wild, to purchase stuff that will be forgotten before the bills arrive in January.

You probably know of someone, perhaps yourself, who has been in some way separated from their income. It can be due to a job layoff, a tragic disability, or any number of other reasons. The loss of one's income can be one of life's most devastating events. But a CF can help.

Two Cases in Point

Meet Tom and Lisa Moore. The Moores live paycheck to paycheck on Tom's salary. There's never enough money. They're habitually late paying their bills but somehow manage to get caught up several times a year. Tom is able to work overtime during tax season, which helps a lot. However, due to downsizing at his firm, Tom is given a two-week notice of his scheduled layoff. Like a batter who's been "dusted" by an opposing pitcher, Tom and Lisa are knocked to the ground emotionally. What will they do? They're one month behind on the mortgage payment, both of their new cars are leased, and Lisa's made reservations for herself and the girls to fly to Florida next week to visit her parents.

They have no sources from which to draw. Tom hasn't been with the firm long enough to warrant severance pay. Their credit cards are maxed out, as is the equity in the house.

Lisa recalls that a preapproved line of credit from a big finance company came in the mail a few days ago. She madly rummages through the trash, finds it, and breathes a sigh of relief. At least they have $3,500. She decides not to bother Tom with the matter because the last thing he needs to worry about is more debt.

Tom spends the next two weeks putting together his resume and sends out hundreds of copies with no particular rhyme or reason. After three incredibly long weeks, Tom finally gets his first unemployment check, but it doesn't begin to cover the stacks of bills growing on the table. Lisa is beside herself with worry, wishes she'd never gone to Florida, has gone through the $3,500 from the finance company, and is about to lose her mind because Tom spends every day pacing and stewing.

The first foreclosure notice arrives three months following Tom's layoff. Creditors call daily. Lisa's stomach is in a knot most of the time. She has one nerve remaining, and it's about shot.

Finally, after four income-less months, Tom receives a job offer. It's not exactly what he'd hoped for and the pay cut will be hard to handle, but it's a job with a paycheck. He jumps at the offer and within two weeks receives his first, albeit smaller, paycheck.

It's been two years since Tom's job change. He's not that happy in his position but has decided to grin and bear it. Lisa has taken a part-time job at the kids' school and hates every minute of it. They've still not recovered from the devastation of the layoff. Their debts are higher than ever, and their credit report is all but ruined. Worst of all, they're no more prepared for a future layoff than they were before.

Meet Greg and Jody Spencer. The Spencers have three children. Jody has a small desktop-publishing business in their home, and Greg is a foreman at the local steel plant. Greg participates faithfully in his company's 401(k) plan, contributing 5 percent of his gross pay into the fund, and the company matches his contributions. In addition, another 10 percent of his pay is deducted and automatically deposited into their online savings account, which has been earning from 3 to 5 percent interest and serves as their contingency fund.

Greg has been at the plant long enough to know that good times come and go. While the chances are fairly slim, he could be laid off. Even if it was temporary, he needs to know they have money set aside to cover the bills.

As a result of deep cuts in defense spending, Greg's company loses the government contract they had for many years. In no time at all, pink slips are distributed, and Greg receives his. But while this is not good news, it is not devastating.

Greg spends the next two weeks dreaming and exploring his options. He and Jody talk about all the things they've wished they could pursue but have rejected because of Greg's job.

They withdraw just the minimum amount needed from their contingency fund to cover their basic living necessities during the time between Greg's last paycheck and his first unemployment check. They supplement the unemployment checks with money from their contingency fund to keep the bills paid and food on the table.

Greg puts together a resume based on his dream of becoming a professional photographer. He includes information on competitions he's won as well as examples of his work. During the next two months, he follows up every possible lead in the area of photography and lands not one but two interviews.

Greg is offered a position as an apprentice with the largest commercial photography company in the city, and he eagerly accepts. The pay is similar to what he'd been making at the plant.

During the first year of Greg's new job, he and Jody are determined to reduce expenses so they can replace the money they took from their contingency fund. They increase their contribution from 10 percent to 15 percent so as to repay the money more quickly.

Greg and Jody did not have a negative reaction to their set of circumstances. In fact, Greg looks back on his layoff as one of the best things that ever happened to him. This blessing disguised as a pink slip opened the doors for him to blend his life's work with his creative passions. They didn't miss a beat in paying their house payment and utility bills. Because they had the peace of mind a contingency fund can bring, they actually had fun during this unexpected time off between jobs.

141

Tom and Lisa, on the other hand, suffered greatly. Their relationship was dealt a blow because Lisa activated that $3,500 loan without Tom's knowledge. Tom became so depressed that Lisa didn't even want to be around him. Their girls became needlessly fearful that they would be homeless. And each month, rather than getting ahead, Tom and Lisa fell further and further behind as their debt grew and grew.

Tom is anything but fond of his job, but he feels hopelessly stuck, and Lisa resents having to work. Tom's layoff greatly altered their lives, and they are much worse off because of it.

A Freedom Account

Expenses that don't occur on a regular monthly basis are often forgotten. When they rise up to remind us of their existence, we often refer to them as emergencies. They're also considered financial crises.

Irregular, intermittent, and unpredictable expenses include things such as insurance premiums, new brakes on the car, veterinarian bills, vacations, clothes, and Christmas, to name a few. They are expenses that vary in amount and don't occur at precisely the same time every month.

My theory is this: Most of us have found a way to handle mortgage or rent payments, grocery bills, utilities, car payments—our monthly expenses. It's all the other things that creep up on us and scare us to death that send us running to the credit cards or some other form of credit. If we could just come up with a way to predict those expenses, we could plan ahead and never be caught off guard again.

I created a management tool called a freedom account. It is an account you create at your bank that is perfectly designed to make sure you are prepared for irregular, intermittent, and unpredictable expenses.

Here are the basic guidelines for creating your own freedom account:

1. Using a year's worth of check registers, credit card statements, and paid receipts, reconstruct the irregular, intermittent, and unpredictable expenses you had to deal with last year such as medical and dental expenses, taxes, insurance premiums, vacations, and Christmas.
2. Divide each amount by twelve. One-twelfth of each expense is what you need to set aside each month in anticipation of these expenses.
3. Open a separate checking account to handle your freedom account.
4. Each month make a deposit for each of the above items.
5. In a notebook, create a separate page for each category or subaccount. Each month enter that month's deposit and calculate a new balance.
6. As irregular, intermittent, and unpredictable expenses come up for which you have set up a subaccount, write out a check from your freedom account to make the payment. Record it on the subaccount page as a debit and calculate the new balance.

Used properly, your freedom account will revolutionize your finances. Being prepared for emergencies, large or small, is great on its own, but it also creates fringe benefits such as less stress, more financial options, and an overall feeling of maturity, responsibility, and well-being.

12

A Financially Confident Woman Knows Her Financial Condition

> The shortest recorded period of time lies between the minute you put some money away for a rainy day and the unexpected arrival of rain.
>
> Jane Bryant Quinn

Becoming a mother to two babies born in quick succession was for me just short of completely overwhelming. All the feeding, cleaning, changing, burping, nurturing, cuddling—it's hard to know if you're doing things right and if the baby is developing correctly. We relied heavily on weighing, measuring, assessing, and testing to tell us how they were doing with growth and development.

Most of our well-baby evaluations revealed that they were on track and making good progress. And when the results were not as glowing, we were grateful for early detection because that allowed for swift intervention. I can tell you we would have been in big trouble had we waited many years to have our boys' growth and development assessed.

Caring for your financial situation is quite similar to raising children. You do what you think is the right thing on a day-by-day basis, but you need regular weighing, measuring, assessing, and evaluating to determine if you are on the right track. Thankfully, you don't have to haul yourself into the office of a professional financial assessor. You can learn to do all the "weighing and measuring" yourself to assess your personal financial situation.

It doesn't matter if you're single or married or whether you handle the finances in your home or not. Every woman needs to possess certain basic financial skills that enable her to balance a checkbook and develop a spending plan, cash flow statement, and net worth statement.

Balance Your Checkbook

I can already hear you say, "Why do I have to do this?!" Look, I of all people know balancing a checkbook can be a rash-inducing assignment, but once you understand the process, you'll wonder why you ever avoided this simple task. Balancing, or reconciling, your checkbook simply means proving that what the bank says you have in your account is correct.

Prior to the digital age, when banks and credit unions offer access to your account online so that you can watch it 24/7, all a person had was a monthly paper statement showing a bank's version of the state of one's account. Does this mean the act of balancing a checkbook is archaic and a big waste of time? I can't fully agree to that because, well, I'm kinda old-fashioned.

We live in an imperfect world. Now and then mistakes happen. More than once in my life my credit union actually credited a deposit to my account that wasn't mine. Had I simply relied on the current balance I saw in my smartphone app, I could have been fooled into thinking I had more money than I did. If you make a mistake or forget to post an ATM withdrawal, debit card purchase, or other transaction in your checkbook register, you may start bouncing checks and incurring penalties.

If you use personal finance software such as Mint, Quicken, or Mvelopes to manage your bank account, you may assume you do not need to balance your account, thinking the software will do this for you. That is a wrong assumption. You still must reconcile at least once a month. The software just makes it easier.

Okay, let's get started.

To me, the hardest thing about a checking account is remembering to write down the amount of a check as it is written. We found duplicate checks to be the solution. Each check has its own carbon copy that remains in your checkbook after you've torn out the check. With this record, you will always know to whom and for how much you wrote each check.

Before you start the reconciling process, make sure you have calculated a current balance in your checkbook that reflects all the checks you've written and the deposits you've made since the last time you balanced your account. Then assemble the following:

1. your checking account statement from the bank
2. canceled checks or photocopies sent by the bank
3. your checkbook register, ATM receipts, debit card transaction receipts, and paycheck stubs
4. checkbook balancing worksheet (it's on page 147)
5. pencil and eraser
6. calculator

Step 1. Sort the deposit slips and checks into two groups. Place ATM deposit slips with the deposits and put cash withdrawal slips, transfers, and payments with the checks.

Step 2. Look at your bank statement and compare the canceled check with the amount of the check as noted on the statement. Banks do make errors now and again. For instance, you might have written a check for $48.26, but the check shows up on your statement as $84.26. Circle or make note of any discrepancies.

Step 3. Go through your checkbook register and check off each check listed on the statement. If a check has not been cashed and therefore does not show up on the statement, list that amount under "checks outstanding."

Step 4. Look on the statement for any bank charges, such as the cost of checks, service fees, or overdraft fees. Enter these bank charges in your checkbook register and deduct the amount just as you would if you'd written a check.

Step 5. Look on the statement for automatic or direct withdrawals you may have authorized, such as insurance payments or investment transfers. Make sure these are deducted in your register just as if you'd written a check.

Step 6. Look for direct deposits (some people have their paychecks, dividends, or Social Security checks deposited directly, and some checking accounts earn interest). Make sure each has been entered into your checkbook register as a credit and added to the balance.

Step 7. Make sure you have entered every ATM withdrawal and debit card transaction into your register and that your statement doesn't contain extras that might belong to someone else.

Okay, now that you've gotten everything together and your checkbook register is current, you're ready to move on to the checkbook balancing worksheet. Most bank statements have a worksheet printed on the back. I can nearly guarantee it won't be as easy to read and as user-friendly as mine, but feel free to proceed with your worksheet of choice. Just fill in the blanks.

Checkbook Balancing Worksheet

My balance according to my checkbook [ ]

These two balances should agree.

My balance according to the bank [ ]

Outstanding Checks
(checks, debit card purchases, and ATM withdrawels that do not appear on my bank statement.)

Date	Chk#	Amt
Total:		

Outstanding Deposits
(Deposits I made but do not appear on my bank statement.)

Date	Amt
Total:	

[ ] Ending balance on bank statement

+

[ ] Plus outstanding deposits

=

[ ] Equals Subtotal

−

[ ] Minus outstanding checks

=

In the off chance your checkbook balance and bank statement balance are not exactly the same, don't panic. Just find the error. Here are some suggestions for finding it quickly.

Is there an error in your addition or subtraction?

Did you deduct all the bank charges from your checkbook balance before you started on the worksheet?

Does the amount you're "out of balance" ring a bell? Does it just happen to be the exact amount of that cash withdrawal you took last week and forgot to write down?

Divide the out-of-balance amount by nine. If the answer is a whole number (nothing behind the decimal point), there's a good chance you transposed a figure. Example: The check was for $8.59, but you wrote down $8.95 in your checkbook.

Did you fail to write down a deposit? (Happy find!)

If you just can't find the error, your bank will be more than happy to. Take your statement, checkbook, and worksheet to the bank. Leaving the mystery unsolved will only set you up for a bigger problem next month.

Develop a Spending Plan

When we were children, we were accountable to grown-ups for just about everything, from making our beds to completing our homework. As we matured, little by little that accountability shifted. By the time we left home, we were no longer accountable to our parents and other authority figures; we were accountable to ourselves. Well, that's the way it's supposed to work. But the process must have a high breakdown rate because too many of us end up accountable to no one for our personal finances.

Let's see how accountable you've been to yourself with your finances. How much did you spend on food last month? Auto repairs? Credit card payments? Late fees? Cab fare? Haven't a clue or even a vague notion? Well, don't feel too bad. Most people have a difficult time coming up with figures for such routine expenses. I suppose denial has something to do with it. If you have no idea what your bank balance is, you don't have to face the reality that you don't have enough to buy a newspaper, let alone cover the cash withdrawal you pulled out of the ATM last night.

Assuming you are sick and tired of living in a financial fog, then you should welcome the bright light that only a precise spending record will turn on in your life. I wouldn't be surprised if such clarity might be a bit intimidating. The truth is not often welcome, especially if it points out problem areas in our lives. You may be hesitant to bring into sharp focus the exact nature of your finances. Whatever your fears, please do not underestimate the value and importance of recording your spending. Knowing the truth really will set you free.

Make a Daily Spending Record

The first step in developing a spending plan is to make a daily spending record for thirty days or one month. This is simply a written account of money spent during a specific day. Writing it down is the only way to find out where all the money goes. If you are married, this is going to require a bit of teamwork. If you have an uncooperative partner, start by becoming accountable to yourself for whatever amount of money you control.

From now on you will look at each month as having four weeks, regardless of what day of the week the first falls on or how many days are in the month: days 1–7 will always be week 1; days 8–14 will always be week 2; days 15–21 will always be week 3; days 22–end of the month will always be week 4. It doesn't matter that the fourth week of every month will have anywhere from six to nine days.

Get a little notebook or small pad of paper. Each day start with a fresh page and put the current date at the top. Each time you spend cash, make a credit card purchase (yes, write it down because you've spent the money even if it doesn't feel that way), or write a check, jot down two entries: what and how much. That's it. One page per day every day. No time off. No endless details and no totals (for now). Given the miracle of twenty-one, this should become a habit in about three weeks.

Daily Spending Record

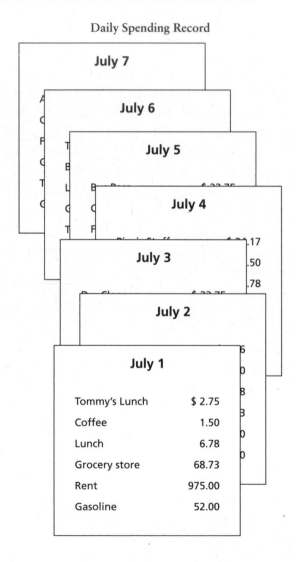

July 1	
Tommy's Lunch	$ 2.75
Coffee	1.50
Lunch	6.78
Grocery store	68.73
Rent	975.00
Gasoline	52.00

In the case of a partnership, both you and your spouse should keep a daily spending record, even if one spouse handles very little of the family income. Remember, this is not an exercise in spying on each other or making sure neither partner has any money to call their own. It is simply an effort to determine where the money goes. This may not need to be a long-term activity (for some it becomes a lifelong habit), but you should do it for at least thirty days in order to develop a spending plan.

A daily spending record has a very specific purpose. It helps you gather the information you need to formulate a weekly spending record. Four weekly records will help you produce your first full monthly spending record.

It's the fringe benefits of this activity that are going to surprise you. If you are true to yourself and diligently write down every dollar, dime, and penny you spend, your spending activities are going to change dramatically. I don't know why. Perhaps recording our spending makes us stop spending unconsciously. Knowing you'll have to write it down makes you think twice before you drop $20 on something you might otherwise have purchased in a moment of impulsiveness.

Make a Weekly Spending Record

You have fixed expenses (car payment, mortgage payment, etc.) and flexible expenses (food, gasoline, utilities, etc.). You need to come up with a list of expenses that are unique to you and your family. Try to be neither too detailed nor too general. Too many categories will be unmanageable. Too few will give you only a vague idea of where your money goes. The average family will likely have fifteen to twenty categories. Looking through your checkbook register or your canceled checks will help you recall expenses you have on a recurring basis.

A weekly spending record is going to bring further clarity because it summarizes your daily spending activities. At the end of week 1, gather the week's spending records (if you are married, ideally you'll have fourteen of these; if you're single, you'll have seven). Using this information, make a simple weekly spending record similar to the illustration.

Weekly Spending Record

Month of January
Week 1 (Days 1–7)

Savings	$100.00
Giving	100.00
Rent	950.00
Groceries	183.57
Food (away from home)	52.73
Telephone	68.74
Gasoline	40.00
Auto oil change	29.95
Clothing	53.87
Property taxes	200.00
School tuition	76.00
Publications	16.45
Gifts (Grandma's birthday)	19.58
Home Depot (household maint.)	58.68
Medical	24.25
Children's school supplies	15.86
Credit card payment	158.00
Other debt payment	75.00
Total	$2,222.68

Determine Average Monthly Income

Regardless of your payroll schedule or the frequency with which you receive other sources of income, next you need to come up with your average monthly income, the number that when multiplied by twelve equals your annual gross income. I prefer to work with a gross figure (before any taxes or other withholding is applied); however, you may be more comfortable working with a net figure, or your actual take-home pay. You decide. Just be consistent once you've made the decision. If you work with a gross figure, include expense categories for money that is withheld from your wages.

Here is a simple formula for determining your average monthly income. If you are paid . . .

weekly: multiply your income by 4.333

biweekly: multiply your income by 2.167

semimonthly: multiply your income by 2

quarterly: divide your income by 3

annually: divide your income by 12

When determining your average monthly income, include all sources such as salary, wages, commission, dividend and interest income, child-support payments, alimony, etc. If you get money on a regular basis, can predict its arrival, and can spend it, it's income.

Make a Monthly Spending Record

Once you have completed daily and weekly spending records for an entire month, you should transfer this information to a monthly spending record. Now the truth is coming into focus. Once you have totaled your entire month's spending activities, subtract this amount from your average monthly income. This total will show you how much you are overspending or under-spending your income.

Keep in mind that this month will not be duplicated every month because of irregular, intermittent, and unpredictable expenses. Repeating this process for the next two months will give you an even clearer picture.

Monthly Spending Record

Category	Week 1	Week 2	Week 3	Week 4	Total
Savings	$100.00	$100.00	$100.00	$100.00	$400.00
Giving	100.00	100.00	100.00	100.00	400.00
Rent	950.00				950.00
Groceries	183.57	237.65	58.00	74.34	553.56
Food (away)	52.73	14.50	5.76	45.85	118.84
Electricity		87.50			87.50
Heating fuel					00.00
Telephone	68.74				68.74
Car payments			279.00	183.00	462.00
Gasoline	40.00	40.00	40.00	40.00	160.00
Auto maint.	29.95		37.50		67.45
Insurance		72.50		22.00	94.50
Clothing	53.87	89.00		12.98	155.85
Property taxes	200.00				200.00
School tuition	76.00				76.00
Publications	16.45				16.45
Gifts	19.58				19.58
Entertainment		25.00		10.50	35.50
Haircuts				17.50	17.50
House maint.	58.68	21.53	15.67		95.88
Medical	24.25				24.25
Children's misc.	15.86		24.00	10.00	49.86
Credit cards	158.00				158.00
Other debt	75.00				75.00
Miscellaneous					—
Totals	$2,222.68	787.68	659.93	616.17	$4,286.46

If you are diligent and continue recording your spending, developing weekly and monthly spending records, something remarkable is bound to happen. You are going to automatically see where your problem with spending lies.

I once received a letter from a woman who shared her astonishment that given her current pace she would spend well over

$1,500 on cappuccino in the coming year. Once she started writing down her daily expenditures, it was clear that, at $3 a cup and sometimes more than once a day, this little treat was quickly destroying her solvency. She saw the big picture, determined that there were other things she'd much rather do with $1,500 each year, and made the decision on her own to make some changes. A budget would not have pointed out her problem. That's the difference between a budget and a plan. I much prefer any title that does not include the word *budget*.

Make a Monthly Spending Plan

The difference between a monthly spending record and a monthly spending plan is a column titled "Plan to Spend." Based on what you spent in the previous month, what do you need to spend next month to make sure your expenses are less than your average monthly income? You decide. This is your spending plan; it's your life.

Monthly Spending Plan

Category	Week 1	Week 2	Week 3	Week 4	Total Spent	Plan to Spend

Category	Week 1	Week 2	Week 3	Week 4	Total Spent	Plan to Spend

_____ Average Monthly Income

_____ Total Actually Spent This Month

_____ Amount Underspent or <Overspent>

Can you get that fast-food amount down a few notches by cooking at home more often? Is there anything you can do to cut that huge heating bill in half? And that entertainment category. Yikes! Is this really where you want that much money to go each month?

If your situation is severe—after cutting back you are still spending more than you earn—you may need to look at some drastic cost-cutting measures, such as moving into less-expensive housing or selling a car. There are only three ways to change this picture: increase income, decrease expenses, or sell assets.

And so you plan for the coming month. On the form for the next month, you fill in the "Plan to Spend" column ahead of time. As the weeks unfold and you fill in your actual spending, all kinds of lights are going to come on. You'll start projecting what will happen at the end of the month if you keep spending the way you are. This is called managing your money, and in time it's going to feel really good. This is how to start taking control of your money instead of letting it control you.

Your Personal Economy

You'd have to be living under a rock not to be aware that the national economy goes through cycles of growth and decline. People get nervous when forecasters predict a recession or the economy slows down. And that's pretty much wasted energy.

Forget the national economy. The only thing you can control is your personal economy. It is not a foregone conclusion that your personal economy will reflect the national economy's ups and downs. In fact, plenty of people see their economic well-being decline while the nation as a whole is doing great, while others make great financial progress when the rest of the nation is facing a major downturn. When you're secure in a good job, it doesn't matter to you if the national unemployment rate is creating gloomy headlines at 5 percent. But everything changes when you are unemployed. It doesn't matter if the national rate is low when you're the one with the pink slip. For you, the unemployment rate is 100 percent.

As difficult as it may be to face the truth of where you are financially, it's the smart thing to do. After all, you'll never figure out how to get where you want to be until you know where you are.

Three important personal economic indicators generally reveal your overall financial condition and predict your financial future: your gross income, your cash flow, and your net worth.

Gross Income

Your gross income is the total income of all household wage earners before taxes, retirement contributions, and other expenses are deducted from your paycheck(s), along with any other sources of income such as dividends and interest. The easiest way to come up with this number is to look at your most current pay stubs and other statements that show any and all income. Once you have your current gross annual income (or you can use a monthly figure if your income is fairly stable), compare this number to your gross income in the same period one year ago.

If you are making at least 2 percent more than you were one year ago, you are just about keeping up with inflation. Your money is losing value through inflation because it takes at least 2 percent more each year to purchase the same goods and services. If your gross income has increased more than 2 percent, you are making financial progress. When gross income falls but does not quickly recover, you need to pay particular attention. This means you may be heading for a personal recession.

Cash Flow

Your cash flow is your gross income for a set period of time—for a month or a year—minus your total outgo for that same period. Your cash flow could sink even while your income increases if your spending is increasing at a faster rate than your income. Seeing the reality of your cash flow can be shocking and quite possibly just the jolt you need to rein in your spending.

Now that you know how to create a monthly spending plan, you're on your way to having all you need to create a cash flow statement. This is a report that shows all the income for the year and all the outgo. What came in and what happened to it?

Businesses rely heavily on cash flow statements in projecting growth and boosting profits. You are no less important than a business, so an annual cash flow statement will become a valuable tool as you better manage your money.

Using the information from your twelve monthly spending records, fill in the cash flow form. Ideally, your income should equal your outgo, which means you've been able to account for every dollar that passed through your hands. Don't panic if you can't be that exact. The fact that you've come this far is remarkable. Besides, I don't know anyone who could be precise to the penny over an entire year. But it's a fine goal, so keep reaching for it.

Cash Flow Statement

As of _____

Income

Gross salaries		
Dividend income		
Interest income		
Savings		
Other		
Total Income		*$

Outgo

Savings		
Giving		
Investments		
Taxes		
Mortgage payments		
Debt payments		
Insurance premiums		
Food		
Transportation		
Clothing/personal care		
Entertainment/vacations		
Medical/dental		
Utilities/household expenses		
Miscellaneous		
Total Outgo		*$

*These two amounts should be the same.

161

Net Worth

Simply put, your net worth is the amount of money you would have left if you sold everything you own (your assets) and used that money to pay off everything you owe (your liabilities). There are only two ways you can improve your net worth: increase assets and decrease liabilities.

Creating your first net worth statement will take some time and effort. I want to encourage you to do this because it will give you amazing insight into many things, such as the way some things lose value quickly. A case in point might be a new vehicle you purchased two years ago that today is worth less than the amount you owe on it.

Your first net worth statement will be your benchmark, a reference point. Next year you will be able to compare your financial picture with this year's statement to see the changes. You should create a net worth statement at least annually. If you are married, your net worth statement should be the financial condition of you as a couple in one joint statement.

Your net worth statement is an important tool because it helps you do the following:

- check and measure your financial progress in relation to your financial goals (think of it as a financial "growth chart")
- make decisions about acquiring assets and taking on liabilities in the future
- estimate how well-off your family would be if you were suddenly taken from them
- determine your need for life and property insurance and adjustments you need to make in your coverage
- estimate what your income will be during your retirement

A net worth statement does not care about income. In fact, there is not even a place to record your annual salary. A net worth statement doesn't care how much you spend on food,

162

clothes, or education. What your statement reveals is how much of your hard-earned income you keep. It confirms the belief that it doesn't really matter how much money you make. What matters is what you do with your money.

There are two major categories on a net worth statement: assets and liabilities—what you own and what you owe. When you deduct what you owe from what you own, the result is your net worth.

Assets

To begin, you need to know the current market value of all your assets. Assets are anything you own of value, including cash or cash equivalents, investments, and things such as your home, cars, and personal possessions of value. Even those things you are in the process of paying off and do not yet own outright are considered assets. You'll probably have to take an inventory to gather the information you'll need. Don't get too detailed, however.

Assets are divided into two categories: appreciating assets and depreciating assets.

Appreciating assets are things you own that become more valuable over time. Everything else is losing value and therefore depreciating. Investments such as retirement accounts and stock market holdings are appreciating assets because they have the likelihood of gaining in value over time. Savings and cash come under the heading of appreciating assets; so does real estate. Certain collectibles appreciate, but be careful here. You want market confirmation of the values you set for your appreciating assets. You may believe your Beanie Baby collection is worth a lot more than what you could realistically sell it for next weekend.

On your net worth statement, list each of your appreciating assets with a corresponding value for each. If your home would sell for $200,000 on today's market and you have a $100,000 mortgage, list it as $200,000 under your appreciating assets. This is also where you should list the current value of your retirement accounts, certificates, stocks, bonds, and mutual funds. To find the current value of your investments, look for market quotes in a current newspaper or by going to a website like Yahoo.com and checking the day's financial markets. You can get the current day's value for each of the stocks and mutual funds you own simply by typing in the ticker symbol, which you can also look up at the site. Use actual cash figures for cash on hand and in checking and savings accounts.

Include money owed to you as an asset, but only if you are certain of repayment. For example, if you lent $1,000 to a friend and he has already repaid $300, enter $700 under appreciating assets.

Other possessions, such as cars, TVs, boats, clothes, jewelry, and household goods, are depreciating assets because, while they have value, they are becoming less valuable with time. Unless your car is a rare collector's item (in which case it would be an appreciating asset), it is worth less today than it was yesterday. In fact, if you bought it new, it was worth 20 percent less the day after you bought it due to depreciation.

Some experts suggest an estimate of $10,000 current market value for personal property including furniture, clothes, tools, and all other household items of a typical two-adult household. You may wish to use that figure or determine your own.

LIABILITIES

Next, list all your debts. When it comes to a net worth statement, debt is debt. We make no differentiation between secured and unsecured debt. Any amount you owe another person or entity should be accounted for under liabilities. These are obligations such as mortgages, home equity loans, car loans, automobile leases, student loans, personal loans, court-mandated child support (up to one year's worth), contracts for things such as wireless devices, gym membership contracts—anything for which you have an obligation to pay. Be honest and exact. If you don't know for sure, call the lender and ask.

Net Worth Statement—Two-Year Comparison

Assets—Appreciating		
Cash in checking	12	1,808
Savings accounts	0	10,000
Retirement 401(k) and IRAs	804	2,765
House	132,000	175,000
Stocks, bonds, funds	0	575
Other	12,000	15,000
Total Appreciating Assets	**$144,816**	**$205,148**

Assets—Depreciating		
Personal property	10,000	10,000
Auto—2004 Chevy Truck	24,000	16,000
Auto—2000 Acura	4,000	1,000
Jet ski	2,300	750
Total Depreciating Assets	**40,300**	**27,750**

Total Assets	**$185,116**	**$232,898**

Liabilities		
Home mortgage	122,000	112,000
HEL (home equity loan)	0	5,000
Student loans	32,000	30,000
Credit card debt	18,900	2,000
Loan from 401(k)	0	0
Loan from parents	4,000	0
Past due utility bills	223	0
Jet ski	745	0
Doctors	1,900	0
Hospitals	545	0
Truck loan	23,000	17,000
Total Liabilities	**−203,313**	**−166,000**

Net Worth	**<$18,197>**	**$66,898**

RESULTS

Finally, subtract your total liabilities from your total assets. The result is your current net worth.

Your net worth tells a story. It doesn't lie; it doesn't deceive. The last number—the bottom line—reveals how much of your income you've managed to keep. If that is a negative number, you've managed to spend more than you've earned, relying on credit to fill in the gap. Or you can think of it this way: You've been spending all you've earned, plus a lot you haven't even earned yet.

What you see on your net worth statement is your financial condition as of today. If you are discouraged by what you see, let me encourage you. You have control over this situation. As helpless or as hopeless as you may feel right now, this is a picture you can change beginning now.

Take another look at your net worth statement. Focus on one of your debts, like a credit card debt. Imagine that you will reduce that balance by $5 when you send your payment tomorrow. That will immediately increase your net worth by $5. Five dollars here, $10 there is the way to change your financial picture. Perhaps the most important thing you can learn from this chapter is this: Reducing debt increases net worth dollar for dollar. A repaid debt is a good investment.

Just as soon as practical, prepare your net worth statement. Do this as accurately as possible. Inflating figures or cheating by excluding liabilities only hurts you. You need to know where you are so that you will be able to measure how you are doing as you begin to debt-proof your life.

You will be creating a benchmark against which to measure your future progress. That is going to have a positive effect on your determination to become a better caretaker of your money.

It is going to be exciting to plot your financial growth. Even your smallest efforts to repay debt and save money are going to count. You'll see.

13

A Financially Confident Woman Gets What She Pays For

Your objective is to reeducate sellers, teach them that your money isn't theirs without your consent. If they've cheated to get your money, don't let them keep it.

Donna McCrohan

It was brilliant. There's no other way to describe the way syndicated talk-show radio host Rich Buhler ended a particularly difficult call. "Just remember this: Always remain a fragrance; never become an odor." Over the years, that little piece of advice has stuck with me like a sock with static cling.

When I was growing up, I didn't fully understand the concept, although I was rebuked again and again for "your attitude," "that tone of voice," and "it's not what you say but the way you say it." As a mother—you know, that time in life when you start saying the things your parents said—I came into full awareness of this concept.

It's not necessarily what we say but the way we say it. One version leaves a fragrance; the other projects an odor. Fragrance leaves us yearning for more, while odors send us running for cover. Time and again since first considering this fragrance/odor thing, I've been able to look back and determine what went wrong—where the negotiations broke down. It wasn't what I said to my parents that was particularly offensive but the way I said it.

Personality traits that I label enthusiasm and zeal can easily be misconstrued as criticism and control. What I say can be taken the wrong way. When that happens, I'm afraid I give off an "odor" that does absolutely nothing to endear me to the person with whom I'm dealing. This concept relates to the subject of getting what you pay for. If you know how to behave with fragrance, charm, and dignity, you'll get the results you deserve every time.

Your Reasonable Expectations

Contrary to what the old rock 'n' roll song says about satisfaction, I believe that with the right attitude, the correct information, and reliable resources, it is possible to be satisfied with your purchase of goods and services. It's all a matter of knowing what to say and how to say it.

As consumers, we have the right to expect quality products and services at fair prices. We have the right to expect sellers to stand behind their products if a problem develops. It's not unreasonable to expect to get what we pay for. We, the faithful consumers, are a necessary part of the economy. And as responsible stewards of the many resources entrusted to us by God, I believe we have an obligation to make sure we get what we pay for.

Confrontation has never been high on my list of things I love to do. In my past, even when I purchased something that turned

168

out to be defective, I would worry that the store owner wouldn't agree with me or wouldn't believe me, insisting that the product was fine when it left the store, so I must have caused the damage. And the idea of returning an item simply because the color turned out to be wrong or I just changed my mind intimidated me beyond belief. Somewhere deep down inside me I just didn't want to give the salesclerk an opportunity to yell at me or announce over the loudspeaker to the entire community that some woman up here has the unmitigated gall to change her mind.

This particular aversion cost me a lot of money over the years. My compulsive nature and propensity to buy everything in sight, particularly if it was on sale (which for a shopaholic always confirms God's blessing on the purchase and his providential supplying of need), coupled with my fear of returning an item were a deadly combination of behaviors. At this point in my life, I'd just as soon not know how many brand new items—some defective, some not—I've given away or thrown out simply because I was too embarrassed to take them back.

The good news is that most sellers make a concerted effort to settle customer complaints in a satisfactory manner. Many even go beyond the minimum required by federal consumer-protection laws, not only because it's the right thing to do but also because it's a great way to keep us as loyal, returning customers.

I have also observed the way financially confident women live, and through mimicking their behaviors in this area of making sure I always get what I pay for, I've changed. I've learned how to practice the habit of reasonable expectation—not with a demanding demeanor or threatening attitude but with a gentle expectation that sellers are not entitled to my money without my full consent.

The more I exercise this new behavior, the more cautious I become at the point of purchase. I make selections more carefully, think things through, and actually take time to make decisions. Because I know the consequences of an inappropriate purchase may include the dreaded return to the store for a refund or acceptable adjustment, making the best decision the first time around has become much more important than it used to be.

A Short History of Consumer Protection

In the late 1800s, increased industrialization in the United States provided the opportunity for many new kinds of businesses to advertise and sell their products nationwide. As you can well imagine, along with this unprecedented growth of business came the issue of consumer problems.

In 1938, when over one hundred people died after using a new liquid sulfa drug, a law was enacted requiring manufacturers to prove the safety of new drugs to the Federal Drug Administration before putting them on the market. World War II diverted attention away from the issue of consumer protection, and it didn't attract interest again until the 1960s. During that decade, new programs to protect the public came into existence and existing programs were improved. In 1967, the Consumer Federation of America formed to serve as an umbrella organization of consumer, cooperative, and labor groups.

About this time, Ralph Nader wrote the book *Unsafe at Any Speed*, and he quickly emerged as the leader of a wide range of reform efforts. Many young people volunteered to work in his organization, and under his leadership they participated in research, writing, and lobbying to improve consumer protection.

During the 1960s and 1970s, many new laws were enacted to protect consumers. Among them were the Motor Vehicle Safety Act (1966), the Truth in Lending Act (1969), the Toy Safety Act (1969), and the Consumer Product Safety Act (1972). Legislation also strengthened the Federal Trade Commission.

Even with an increase in consumer protectionism and aware-ness, too many of us seem to accept that time is more important than money—that it's better to be cheated out of a few bucks than to waste time going after them. Most of us, if we complain at all, do so to friends and neighbors, but we usually let the guilty company off the hook because it's simply not worth the bother. According to Technical Assistance Research Programs, only 4 percent of us let a business know when we're dissatisfied with its product or service.[1]

But times are changing. Because of a rough economy and new trends toward frugality, people are more anxious to exercise their rights for fairness.

Complaining with Fragrance

Probably the most important part of getting what you pay for involves keeping your receipts in an organized fashion. It's not as difficult as you might imagine. Any method will do, provided you can easily put your hands on the receipt you need. If something you purchased came with an owner's manual or paperwork, staple the receipt to the front. Always take a moment to write on the receipt a brief description of the item, since many receipts carry only a stock number or an abbreviation that may be com-pletely indecipherable six months from now. Receipts should be kept for at least a year and longer for goods or services that have a reasonable life expectancy of a longer period of time.

Think of the problem-resolution process as a pyramid with a set of ascending stairs. Most problems are readily resolved at the ground level, where the pyramid is the largest. Some situ-ations may require you to climb up a step or two, while more difficult situations may require you to go much closer to the top. However, the times you will have to climb even close to the top of the pyramid will likely be few.

When dealing with a salesperson or representative, always bear in mind that the person deserves your highest respect. He or she has the right to be treated as a person with intelligence and feelings, a person who may very well be working under difficult conditions with an unreasonable supervisor or a person who occasionally has a bad day just as you do. Be reasonable and don't be rude. This stranger with whom you are dealing may very well be the visitor sitting beside you in church next Sunday!

Before beginning the complaint-resolution process, have the following things clear in your mind:

- the exact nature of the problem
- how you wish it to be remedied
- a specific time frame in which you expect the problem to be completely resolved
- your next step if you are unable to find resolution at this level

Here are some other principles to follow.

Principle: Take care of problems before leaving the store or while the service person or contractor is still on the job. Perhaps you discover before leaving the restaurant that the waitress made a mathematical error in your bill, or the painter missed a section of baseboard in the hall bathroom. Whatever the problem, take care of it prior to making full payment.

Principle: Approach the highest-ranking employee with your problem and with dignity and grace seek a satisfactory resolution. If this doesn't work, ask for the name and location of the regional manager or a phone number for customer service. Record the name and title of the person with whom you've been dealing along with the date of the confrontation. When approaching a person, be careful how you're dressed. People do make snap judgments based on appearance. This alone might influence what they believe to be the value in keeping you as a customer, to say nothing of the legitimacy of your problem. This is not the time to look like a mess.

Principle: The next level is the telephone call. Before you make the call, rehearse the facts of your situation. Don't dump on the receptionist. Try to speak with the highest-ranking person at this location. If you are not successful at this level, record the name and title of the person(s) with whom you spoke and the date. If you're successful in having your complaint resolved, ask the person to put the resolution in writing and mail it to you. If this is not forthcoming, follow up with a letter outlining your understanding of the terms of the agreement and a summary of the conversation.

Principle: If your complaint has not been resolved by now, a letter is your next course of action. Letters are great because you can collect your thoughts and arrange them orderly and logically. You have a record of what you've said, and no one can interrupt. Be sure to include a clear and simple statement of the problem, how you've attempted a resolution to date, the resolution you expect, and the date by which you expect it to be accomplished. This letter can be sent via email. If you prefer regular mail, a printed letter is preferable; however, a neatly handwritten letter can be just as effective.

In the letter, include your name, address, and phone number. Make your letter brief and to the point. Include all important facts about your purchase, including the date and place where you made the purchase and any information you can give about the product, such as serial or model numbers. State exactly what you want done about the problem and how long you are willing to wait to get it resolved. Be reasonable. Include photocopies of all documents regarding your problem. Avoid writing an angry, sarcastic, or threatening letter. The person reading your letter probably was not responsible for your problem but may be very helpful in resolving it. Keep a copy of your letter.

Here is a sample letter.

Your address
Date

Appropriate person
Company name
Address

Last week I purchased a [name of product, including serial and model number]. I made this purchase at [location, date, and other pertinent information].

Unfortunately, your product has not performed satisfactorily because [describe problem with product]. I would appreciate your [state specific action you desire].

Enclosed are copies of my records [receipts, guarantees, warranties, canceled checks, contracts, and any other necessary documentation].

I am looking forward to your reply and resolution of my problem. I will wait three weeks before seeking third-party assistance. Contact me at the above address or by phone at (home, office, or cell number).

Sincerely,
Your name and signature

Whenever it's important to prove that you sent something or sent it by a certain date, invest a few extra dollars for certified or registered mail.

Keep a good paper trail from the beginning. This means keeping copies of receipts, your letters, letters you've received, canceled checks, and so on. Notes are valuable as well.

If you do not receive full satisfaction, you need to seek third-party assistance. I suggest you contact your state's Consumer Protection Office, which you can easily find on the internet by searching "Consumer Protection Office" and your state. You as a consumer are well protected by laws that are meant to prevent fraud and provide consumers with an advocate.

I can't think of a better way to become good stewards of the resources we have than by making sure each dollar spent is spent well. By eliminating purchasing mistakes and following up when we are truly not satisfied, we will dramatically affect the bottom line of our financial statements. So be brave, become a documentation fiend, and always deal fragrantly.

14

A Financially Confident Woman Has Eyes for the Future

SMART. This easy-to-remember acronym describes
the characteristics of goal-setting: Specific, Measur-
able, Attainable, Realistic, and Time sensitive.

Jan Cullinane

My heart was broken when I finished reading a letter from
Betty. She related how she and her husband, both octogenar-
ians, struggle from one day to the next—not because of physical
limitations but because of their financial disabilities. They led
a very affluent lifestyle during their younger years and just assumed, along with millions of their peers, that everything would
work out once they retired. Now that they are trying to exist
on their Social Security benefits, they've had a rude awakening.

They are still making payments on their home because they
failed to pay off their mortgage during their years of employment, and they are carrying tremendous credit card debt as a
result of trying to survive day to day. Their dream was that when

they retired they'd travel. They would pursue hobbies and do all the things they put off during the years they were raising a family and building careers.

Because Betty and her husband are too old to be employed, too unemployed to qualify for more credit, too well-off to receive public assistance, and too proud to turn to their children for help, they have no options. I could feel the tears between the lines as she begged me to warn others of the need to prepare well for retirement. "At the time of life when we should be enjoying ourselves the most, we're sitting at a dead-end waiting to die."

Betty's letter became a personal wake-up call for Harold and me. I'll admit it. Retirement was not something on which I chose to dwell. It sounded so far away! Why should we worry about it now? There will be plenty of time to prepare later, I argued. And then I was hit by this truth: The winter season of my life will arrive on time, whether I'm prepared or not. Clearly, being prepared beats the alternative.

Planning for the future has filled me with excitement and wonder—excitement because of all the resources available, and wonder as to why I didn't start sooner.

The bad news is that increasing life expectancies mean most people will outlive their retirement dollars. The good news is that running out of money is rarely a problem for the wise steward who plans ahead and anticipates retirement.

A Second Lifetime to Enjoy

We are certainly among the most fortunate in the history of the world. A woman's life expectancy has nearly doubled over the last century. That's like getting the gift of a second lifetime. As American women, we can expect to live nearly one-third more years in retirement than men of the same age. And we have the knowledge and resources available to make sure we are in the best of health in order to enjoy those extra years. But don't underestimate the fact that making your second lifetime live up to your dreams is going to take a good deal of planning, and the sooner the better.

Your Probable Life Span

Of course, none of us knows how long we will live, but we can make some educated predictions based on statistics and probabilities. Your insurance agent or a simple Google search will help you locate a current mortality table. Using your present age, health, and physical condition, you can predict how many years you will live.

Our days are numbered—no one but God knows how long we have to live—but here's the bottom line: You do not want to outlive your money.

Your Projected Retirement Income

The first place to start in projecting your retirement income is the Social Security Administration. Go to SSA.gov and click on "My Social Security," or call 1-800-772-1213 to request your Social Security statement—a concise, easy-to-read personal record of the earnings on which you have paid Social Security taxes during your working years and a summary of the estimated benefits you and your family may receive as a result of those earnings. This is important for several reasons:

- You'll be able to see if all your employment has been included in your account.
- You'll have an opportunity to correct any errors by resubmitting proof of earnings (the agency seems to have a very high goof rate).
- You'll be able to project your Social Security benefits in retirement if you continue contributing at your present rate.

179

We Will Outlive the Men

Statistically speaking, if you have a man in your life, you are going to outlive him. That makes it likely that at some point you will be solely responsible for your support, your finances, and your care. Get used to the idea. Women outlive men.

Now that we have that straight, let's boil your needs down to just two categories: documents and money. You will need both.

The Documents You Will Need

A Will

While you absolutely need a will, in the big picture, having a will is only slightly better than having nothing when it comes to preparing for your future. But you must start here. The purpose of a will is to tell your heirs and the government how you want your estate (the sum total of what you leave on earth) distributed to your loved ones after your death. Your will also says whom you want to become the legal guardian of your minor children. If you die without a will, the laws of the state will decide all of the above for you—including who will care for your minor children.

A Revocable Living Trust

A will and a trust go hand in hand—you need both. A living trust allows your assets to be passed to your heirs without going through the often expensive, confusing, and long process of probate, in which the state settles your affairs and distributes your assets. That it is revocable means you can change it any time you want. It's not set in stone, but it is in effect. Your revocable living trust also needs to contain an incapacity clause, which allows the trustee you select to make your financial decisions if you do not die but for some reason become incapacitated.

A Durable Power of Attorney for Health Care

This is a document in which you name a person you wish to make your health care and medical decisions if you become unable to do this for yourself. We are not talking just old age here. You could be hit by a bus this afternoon, rendering you incapable of making decisions for a period of time or for much longer. A durable power of attorney gives a person your permission to act on your behalf.

The quickest way to get all three documents (or, if you have some of them already, to get them reviewed) is to make an appointment with an attorney. Ask friends or relatives for a recommendation.

There are also do-it-yourself options. I highly recommend Nolo Press (Nolo.com), a terrific resource that produces do-it-yourself legal books and software that reduce the need for people to hire lawyers for simple legal matters such as making wills.

The Money You Will Need

For most women, retirement holds a great deal of mystery. And for those who do not work outside the home, it can be worse than that.

Where will you get your income if your spouse stops working for any number of reasons? If you have worked all your life, are you guaranteed a retirement income? Will Social Security provide the income you need?

Uncertainty about the future is common among women, but that does not have to be the case for you. You can become certain and financially confident about the years that lie ahead. This requires two things: knowledge and action. The longer you have to save, the less money you will need to contribute because of compounding interest (chap. 7). But you should save early, save often, and save consistently.

The Pretax Advantage

Whether you know it as gross or net, pretax or after-tax, you know that when you get a paycheck what you see in your hand is not the same amount of money you earned. What you earned is the gross amount; what you get is known as net or after-tax dollars. The difference? Taxes and all the withholding required by the federal and state government.

One of the best gifts you will ever get from the government is the provision that allows you to save and invest for retirement using pretax dollars.

Just for illustration purposes, let's say you earn $1,000 gross per week. Of course, you get something closer to $750 after taxes or about 75 cents for each dollar earned.

However, if you are willing to save your money in a qualified savings plan, the government allows you to save pretax dollars. They say something like, "If you put that $1 into a qualified retirement account, we'll let you invest and benefit from the 25 cents that belong to us, and when you retire, we'll take those 25 cents then." That's the simplified version, but it gives you a good idea of how a retirement savings plan works.

Your ability to invest your money before taxes are withheld is huge. This is your ace in the hole, the secret for how you will be able to build a retirement nest egg—provided you keep your hands off the money as it grows. But you need to know where to find these qualified accounts and how to set up your retirement savings.

A Retirement Plan at Work

If you are employed, chances are your employer offers a retirement plan. Corporations offer 401(k) plans; nonprofits such as schools, hospitals, and churches offer 403(b) plans. Other plans go by the acronyms TSA (tax-sheltered annuity) and TSP (thrift savings plan). Which type of retirement plan your employer offers is not important right now. That you are signed up is what matters. Do so immediately if you haven't already. For now, I will refer to all pretax retirement plans as 401(k)s.

As of this writing, the most you can invest in your 401(k) is $17,500 per year unless you are over fifty years old, in which case you can save an additional catch-up amount of $5,500 for a total of $23,000. If you are married, both you and your spouse may be able to put these pretax dollars into your respective employers' 401(k) plans.

Employer Match

Here's another reason you need to sign up now for your employer's retirement plan: employer match. Many companies contribute some of their money to your account either as a flat-out gift or by matching the amount you contribute. This money does not count toward the amount you are allowed to contribute each year. You do not pay taxes on this money until you retire or you take it out of your account.

Employers are not required to offer a contribution, so find out the terms of your company's plan. If your employer does offer to match a portion of your contribution and you are not accepting it, you are walking away from free money. This is just one more reason to find out as soon as possible which retirement plans are available to you.

Retirement Saving on Your Own

There are ways you can get in on the pretax savings benefit if you are not employed or simply do not want to put all your eggs into your company's retirement plan. If the latter, I strongly suggest that you participate at least to the matching point so that you do not leave money on the table. If you do not work outside your home, you can and should still contribute to a retirement account.

183

There are several types of qualified individual retirement accounts (IRAs) that you can set up, invest in, and manage on your own. The number of pretax dollars you can contribute each year depends on whether your employer offers a plan at work and how much money you earn each year.

A traditional IRA is similar to a 401(k) in that you invest pretax dollars. When it's time to withdraw money during retirement, you must pay taxes on the money that was not previously taxed as well as on the gain. The thought is that you will likely be in a lower tax bracket at that time than you are in now during your earning years, so you will come out ahead.

A Roth IRA works differently, but in a beneficial way. With a Roth IRA, you contribute after-tax dollars. No break there. But here's where it gets beneficial. When you withdraw the money, you will not have to pay taxes on any of it. None. Nada. This is huge, especially for those of you who will be starting early, contributing regularly, and allowing the miracle of compounding interest to kick in.

Nonqualified Investments

A "qualified" investment is a plan or a program approved by the IRS that allows you to invest pretax dollars or has some other approved benefit like that of a Roth IRA. You are not limited to qualified investments. You can and probably will invest in many other ways once you have maxed out your qualified investment options.

Where to Get Started

To get started, go online or call a reputable brokerage company that offers retirement accounts and ask to speak with a customer service representative. Here are two companies for your consideration: T. Rowe Price (TRowePrice.com; 1-800-541-6066) and Vanguard (Vanguard.com; 1-800-523-1036). Tell the representative you are interested in opening an individual retirement account and you need to know the limitations and qualifications to do so. At this time, Vanguard requires a minimum of $3,000 to open an account, while T. Rowe Price will open an account for you provided you agree to a $50 automatic deposit each month.

Get a list of questions together, then pick up the phone. Your confidence will soar with each new thing you learn about investing money now for your retirement later.

PART 4

BECOMING A FINANCIALLY CONFIDENT WOMAN

15

A Six-Week Plan of Action

Little drops of water wear down big stones.

Russian proverb

Once you do something twenty-one consecutive times, whether it's exercising, learning an instrument, or practicing new behaviors with money, you will be well on your way to establishing a new habit. Another cycle of twenty-one repetitions will make the behavior a lifelong behavior.

You will be able to take the following guidelines and apply them to your particular set of circumstances. Six weeks is going to give you a good start toward establishing important new habits.

I am a believer in the value of journaling. I recommend that the next six weeks include intensive writing on your part. Find a notebook or a journal that you can keep in a private and secure place.

It's also time to start keeping a daily spending record. Think of this as counting—counting what comes in and what goes out. The journey to financial clarity begins simply by counting. Start

189

right away regardless of where you are in the calendar month and continue every day for the next six weeks (at the very least). Follow the instructions in chapter 12 for keeping a daily spending record, a weekly spending record, and a monthly spending record. You will have an opportunity at some point during this time to prepare your first monthly spending plan.

Week One: Choose Abstinence and Commitment

Abstinence. No, you haven't stumbled into a twelve-step recovery program. Not that I have anything against the twelve-step programs. In fact, for those who have severe spending problems, Debtor's Anonymous is helpful.

Abstinence simply means to keep oneself back, to refrain voluntarily. Abstinence is the primary tool for getting out of debt. For those who have unsecured debt, voluntarily abstaining from incurring any new debt for the next six weeks will be a challenge indeed. To begin, separate yourself from the credit cards. At the very least, move them from your wallet or purse to a place in your home where they will be secure.

While it is not advisable for you to cancel credit card accounts on which you carry a balance (the company would likely raise your interest rate to the max), you can "close" these accounts to yourself. Put one all-purpose credit card in a safe place. Or freeze it in a container of water. Keep this credit card "safe" in your freezer. You'll know where the card is, and you'll also feel pretty silly waiting for it to thaw so you can make an impulsive purchase. Then cut up all the others. It's not going to be easy, but you need to do it if for no other reason than to affirm your commitment to get out of debt.

Abstinence is a simple tool, but do not underestimate it. You may want to devote a section of your journal to abstinence and start listing and writing about other things you will refrain from

190

doing. Ask God to bring to your mind those habits that are hindering your walk of faith and journey to financial freedom.

Commitment. In your journal, make a written commitment to the amount of money you will begin giving and the amount you will pay to yourself. Select a savings vehicle (savings account, sugar bowl, mutual fund) into which you will deposit your savings.

Week Two: Explore Your Belief System

In your journal, write down your fundamental beliefs about money. Refer to chapter 4 to see if any of the beliefs described there strike a chord.

Make a heading titled "My Money Training." Write your memories of the way money was dealt with in your family. Follow this with "My Adult Money Beliefs." How did events from your childhood shape what you think about money today? The more you write, the sooner you'll see a connection between what you learned about money and how you behave with it today.

Answer the following questions as a way of getting in touch with your money beliefs:

- How much money did your family have?
- Were you poor? Rich?
- Have you since discovered that your family was richer (or poorer) than you thought when you were a child?
- When you really wanted something as a child, whom did you ask? Why?
- Did you have about the same, more, or less money than your childhood friends?
- Whose job was it to earn the money for your family?
- Whose job was it to spend the money?
- Who made the financial decisions?

191

What false beliefs, if any, did you find in your personal search? Write them down and commit to removing them from your life by replacing them with solid values. What new money attitudes will be an outward manifestation of these values?

Week Three: Take Stock

This week prepare a written inventory of your financial matters.

Debts. For each non-mortgage debt you have, write down the following about that debt:

- What is the current total outstanding balance?
- What is the interest rate?
- What is the current minimum monthly payment?

If you continue making only the minimum payment each month and incur no new debt, how many monthly payments will you have to make until the debt is completely paid?

Do some soul-searching in this exercise. Think back to debts you might have but that you've tried to forget, like that $1,000 you borrowed from your sister five years ago. You need to pay it back. Write it down.

Assets. Make a list of the things you own that have a market value. Be as detailed as you want.

Week Four: Find Your Balance

By now you should have received a bank statement for your checking account. Refer to chapter 12 and balance it following the instructions. If it takes all week, so what? Cut yourself a little slack and stick with it. It will balance.

Next, prepare your cash flow statement. If you do not have information for the past year (I would be very surprised if you do, to be quite frank), prepare this statement for the past week or two.

Finally, prepare your net worth statement to determine your current net worth. In the event you have a negative net worth, meaning you owe more than you own, don't do anything rash. Just face the truth and commit to getting that situation reversed as soon as possible.

Week Five: Formulate a Get-Out-of-Debt Plan

Using the information from last week, make a written plan as to how you are going to pay each of your debts in full. If you do not add to your debts and begin a systematic repayment plan, full repayment will happen more quickly than you might imagine. Don't be discouraged—be excited! You've taken a major step toward financial confidence.

Go to DebtProofLiving.com to see a demonstration of my Rapid Debt-Repayment Plan®. Members have full access to the RDRP Calculator, which is a cinch to use. Just input all your unsecured debts, hit "calculate," and out comes your unique repayment plan.

Week Six: Focus on the Future

This week is all about future thinking. Your assignment is to make sure you have a valid and current will, a revocable living trust (if your attorney or your own independent research determines this is advisable), and a power of attorney document signed, witnessed, and in a safe place.

This week is also the time to explore your employer-provided retirement plan and the steps you need to take to join it. If you are already participating, review the plan to make sure you are on track. Or get busy opening an IRA or a Roth IRA with a regular monthly deposit.

Conclusion

Hard work is worthwhile,
but empty talk will make you poor
Proverbs 14:23

Our time together has just about come to a close. I don't know about you, but I'm excited! In the course of writing this book, I kept beside the keyboard a pad on which I jotted down new habits I want to learn. My own belief system has been refined and enhanced. I have a lot of work ahead of me, and I'm ready to get started.

No matter what your particular calling in life right now— whether you're a wife, a mother, a professional, or all three— you're a woman both wonderful and unique. And you hold in your hands the basics for becoming a financially confident woman. But we have touched only the tip of the personal finance iceberg here.

First, you need to join me at DebtProofLiving.com. Next, go to EverydayCheapskate.com and sign up to receive a free daily email message from me. This will keep us connected and you on track, taking your newly found financial confidence to the next level.

The timing of your life, like you, is also unique. The time was right for you to read this book; the time was right for me to write it. God has wonderful plans for both of us. I pray that as you change and grow you will embrace the new challenges that will present themselves and that those opportunities will develop excellence in your life like you've never known before.

Write to me and tell me about it. I would love to hear from you.

Mary Hunt
mary@debtproofliving.com

Notes

Introduction

1. Allianz Insurance, "Women, Money, and Power Study: Empowered and Underserved," 2013, https://www.allianzlife.com/retirement/retirement_insights /women_money_power.aspx and https://www.allianzlife.com/Variable/content /public/Literature/Documents/ENT-1462-N.pdf.

Chapter 2: Where Is It Written "Women Don't Do Money"?

1. www.forbes.com/sites/work-in-progress/2010/07/28/women-making -economic-strides-and-not-slowing-down/

2. Allianz Insurance, "Women, Money, and Power Study: Empowered and Underserved," 2013, https://www.allianzlife.com/retirement/retirement_insights/ women_money_power.aspx.

3. http://www.cbpp.org/cms/?fa=view&id=3261.

4. http://www.ssa.gov/pressoffice/basicfact.htm.

5. http://www.experian.com/assets/live-credit-smart/images/6734-gender-trends -infographic-rgb-final-v.pdf.

6. http://www.huffingtonpost.com/visualnewscom/men-vs-women-whos-saving -and-whos-spending_b_3714079.html.

7. http://www.aoa.gov/aoaroot/aging_statistics/profile/2010/docs/2010profile .pdf.

8. http://business.financialpost.com/2012/04/07/women-going-it-alone/.

9. http://www.forbes.com/sites/meghancasserly/2013/09/19/the-geography -of-the-gender-pay-gap-womens-earnings-by-state/.

10. https://www08.wellsfargomedia.com/downloads/pdf/press/4q13pr-wells -fargo-middle-class-retirement-survey.pdf.

Chapter 7: A Financially Confident Woman Is a Saver

1. Alvin Danenberg, *21½ Easy Steps to Financial Security* (Chicago: Publications International, 1995), 50–57.
2. I may be challenged by math, but give me a calculator and I'm good to go! Here's the one I used to figure out Chris's compounding interest wealth: http://www.globalrph.com/davesfv.htm.

Chapter 9: A Financially Confident Woman Says No to Unsecured Debt

1. "The Plastic Safety Net: 2012," http://www.demos.org/publication/plastic-safety-net.
2. http://visual.ly/2012-us-credit-card-usage-statistics, http://www.creditcards.com/credit-card-news/credit-card-industry-facts-personal-debt-statistics-1276.php, http://www.nerdwallet.com/blog/credit-card-data/average-credit-card-debt-household/.
3. Jeffrey Dew, Sonya Britt, and Sandra Huston, *Examining the Relationship between Financial Issues and Divorce*, http://onlinelibrary.wiley.com/doi/10.1111/j.1741-3729.2012.00715.x/abstract; *Family Relations*, 61, no. 4 (October 2012): 615–28.

Chapter 10: A Financially Confident Woman Lives below Her Means

1. http://news.byu.edu/archive13-aug-highheels.aspx.

Chapter 13: A Financially Confident Woman Gets What She Pays For

1. www.refresher.com/archives/!nrfourpercent.html, returnonbehavior.com/2010/10/50-facts-about-customer-experience-for-2011.

Glossary

PITI, ARM, FICO, grace period, HELOC, Fannie Mae, Freddie Mac. Do you know what these financial terms mean? You should, and nothing will boost your financial confidence more than having a working knowledge of each one, plus a few others as well.

Following are the most important financial terms you need to know. Learn one a day—or a week—simply by copying it to an index card or to your computer's screen saver. With one important term at a time, you will increase your FIQ (financial intelligence quotient). In fact, I think you're getting more confident by the minute.

adjustable rate mortgage (ARM). A home loan in which the interest rate is changed periodically based on a standard financial index. ARMs offer lower initial interest rates with the risk of rates increasing in the future. In comparison, a fixed rate mortgage (FRM) offers a higher rate that will not change for the length of the loan. ARMs often have caps on how much the interest rate can rise or fall.

alias. A note on your credit report that indicates other names used for your financial accounts. Sometimes marked as "Also Known As" or "AKA." This can include maiden names or variations on the spelling and format of your full name.

amortization. The process of gradually repaying a debt with regularly scheduled payments.

AnnualCreditReport.com. The official website for obtaining free credit report disclosures from the credit bureaus Equifax, Experian, and Trans Union. You have the right to request a credit report online, by phone, or by mail for free once every twelve months under FACT Act regulations. This free service does not include credit scores or any credit-monitoring services.

annual fee. A charge sometimes required by credit card companies for use of an account. Annual fees range between $15 to $500 a year and are most common with rewards cards or cards for subprime borrowers.

annual percentage rate (APR). The interest rate being charged on a debt, expressed as a yearly rate. Credit cards often have several APRs—one for purchases, one for cash advances, and one for balance transfers. Some lenders may increase the APR if a payment is late.

application fee. The amount a lender charges to process loan application documents. Quality lenders do not charge these fees (though they may charge other fees).

appraisal fee. The amount charged to deliver a professional opinion about how much a property is worth. For a standard home or condominium, this fee is usually $200 to $500.

appraised value. An educated opinion as to how much a property is worth. An appraiser considers the price of similar homes in the area, the condition of the home, and the features of the property to estimate the value.

asset. An item of cash value owned by a person. Assets can include homes, cars, boats, savings, and investments.

authorized user. Anyone who uses your credit cards or credit accounts with your permission. More specifically, someone who has a credit card from your account with their name on it. An authorized user is not legally responsible for the debt and will not get credit score benefit from it. However, the account may appear on their credit report.

average daily balance. The method used to calculate credit card interest due on the outstanding balance each month. An average daily balance is determined by adding each day's balance and then dividing that total by the number of days in a billing cycle. The average daily balance is then multiplied by a card's monthly periodic rate, which is calculated by dividing the annual percentage rate by 12. A card with an annual rate of 18 percent would have a monthly periodic rate of 1.5 percent. If that card had a $500 average daily balance, it would yield a monthly finance charge of $7.50.

balance transfer. The process of moving all or part of the outstanding balance on one credit card to another account. Card issuers sometimes offer teaser rates to encourage balance transfers to their cards and apply balance transfer fees to discourage you from transferring your balance to another card.

balloon loan. A loan in which the payments don't pay off the principal in full by the end of the term. When the loan term expires (usually after five to seven years), the borrower must pay a balloon payment for the remaining amount or refinance. Balloon loans sometimes include convertible options that allow the remaining amount to automatically be transferred into a long-term mortgage. See also *convertible ARM.*

bankruptcy. A proceeding that legally releases a person from repaying a portion of or all debts owed. Bankruptcy damages one's credit report for seven to ten years.

beacon score. A specific credit score developed by Equifax. There are thousands of slightly different credit-scoring formulas used by bankers, lenders, creditors, insurers, and retailers. Scores can vary based on how the formula evaluates credit data.

biweekly mortgage. A mortgage that schedules payments every two weeks instead of the standard monthly payment. The twenty-six biweekly payments are each equal to one-half of a monthly payment. The result is that the mortgage is paid off sooner.

borrower. The individual who is requesting a loan and who will be responsible to pay it back.

cardholder. The person who is issued a credit card and any authorized users.

cardholder agreement. The written statement that gives the terms and conditions of a credit card account. The cardholder agreement is required by Federal Reserve regulations. It must include the annual percentage rate, the monthly minimum payment formula, the annual fee if applicable, and the cardholder's rights in billing disputes. Changes in the cardholder agreement may be made, with written advance notice, at any time by the issuer. Rules for imposing changes vary from state to state, but the rules that apply are those of the home state of the issuing bank, not the home state of the cardholder.

cash advance. A cash loan from a creditor, usually by using a credit card at an ATM, or a loan advance on a paycheck. These loans include special interest rates charged on the amount of the advance.

cash advance fee. A charge by a bank for using credit cards to obtain cash. This fee can be stated in terms of a flat per-transaction fee or a percentage of the amount of the cash advance. For example, the fee may be expressed as follows: 2 percent/$10. This means that the cash advance fee will be either 2 percent of the cash advance amount or $10, whichever is greater.

cash-out refinance. A new mortgage for an existing property in which the amount borrowed is greater than the amount of the previous mortgage. The difference is given to the borrower in cash when the loan is closed.

chapter 7 bankruptcy. A type of consumer bankruptcy in which a person's responsibility for their debts is cleared entirely. With this kind of bankruptcy, a person is not required to pay back debts owed before filing. Chapter 7 bankruptcy filing records remain on a credit report for ten years, and the record of each account included in a filing will remain on a report for seven years.

chapter 11 bankruptcy. A complex type of bankruptcy usually filed by businesses that wish to restructure their debts.

chapter 13 bankruptcy. A type of bankruptcy in which the consumer must pay off some of their debts over time. Chapter 13 bankruptcy filing records remain on a credit report for seven years from the discharge date or ten years from the filing date if it is not discharged. Each account included in the filing will remain on a report for seven years.

charge-off. When a creditor or a lender writes off the balance of a delinquent debt, no longer expecting it to be repaid. A charge-off is also known as a bad debt. Charge-off records remain on a person's credit report for seven years and will harm their credit score. After a debt is charged off, it can be sold to a collections agency.

ChexSystems. A credit-reporting company that tracks banking history and provides this data to banks when a person applies for a new checking account. Negative records, such as bounced checks, can be kept in their database for up to five years. If there are errors on your ChexSystems record, you can contact the company to submit a dispute.

closing costs. The amount charged to a consumer when they are transferring ownership or borrowing against a property. Closing costs include lender, title, and escrow fees and usually range from 3 to 6 percent of the purchase price.

collateral. An asset or property used as security against a loan. If the borrower defaults, the lender agrees to take the collateral as payment for the loan. If the value of the collateral is not equal to or greater than the outstanding amount of the loan, the borrower may be found liable for the deficient amount.

collections. When a business sells a debt for a reduced amount to an agency in order to recover the amount owed. Credit card debts, medical bills, cell phone bills, utility charges, library fees, and video store fees are often sold to collections. Collection agencies attempt to recover past-due debts by contacting the borrower via phone and mail. Collection records can remain on a credit report for seven years from the last 180-day late payment on the original debt. Your rights are defined by the Fair Debt Collection Practices Act.

combined loan-to-value ratio. The total amount one is borrowing in mortgage debts divided by the home's fair market value. Someone with a $50,000 first mortgage and a $20,000 equity line secured against a $100,000 house would have a CLTV ratio of 70 percent.

commitment fee. A fee paid by a borrower to a lender in exchange for a promise that the lender will lend money on certain terms for a specified period. Usually charged in order to extend a loan approval offer for longer than the thirty- to sixty-day standard period. Quality lenders don't usually charge these fees.

conforming loan. A mortgage that meets the requirements for purchase by Fannie Mae and Freddie Mac. Requirements include size of the loan, type, and age. Current loan size limits for single-family homes range from $200,000 to $400,000. Loans that exceed the conforming size are considered jumbo mortgages and usually have higher interest rates.

convenience checks. Checks provided by a credit card company that a person can use to access their available credit. These checks often have different rates and terms than standard credit card charges. Frequently, the terms are not printed with the checks and the only way to know what they are is to call the phone number enclosed.

convertible ARM. An adjustable rate mortgage that can be converted to a fixed rate mortgage under specified conditions.

cosigner. An additional person who signs a loan document and takes equal responsibility for the debt. A borrower may want to use a cosigner if their credit or financial situation is not good enough to qualify for a loan on their own. A cosigner is legally responsible for the loan, and the shared account will appear on that person's credit report. Having a cosigner is helpful only if the cosigner's credit or financial standing is better than that of the primary borrower.

credit bureaus. Also known as credit-reporting agencies (CRAs), these companies collect information from creditors and lenders about consumer financial behavior. This data is then provided to businesses that want to evaluate how risky it would be to lend money to a potential borrower. Once a low-tech system of regional credit-reporting agencies, the industry is now consolidated into the three national credit bureaus: Equifax, Experian, and TransUnion.

credit counseling. A service that helps consumers repay their debts and improve their credit. Usually nonprofit companies, most of these agencies offer helpful and affordable services. Consumers should be aware that there are also credit counseling agencies that are expensive, ineffective, and even damaging to a client's credit. Consumers should carefully review a company's reputation and services before signing up. See also *credit repair.*

credit file. Another term for a credit report. The term *credit file* is generally used to indicate the full record of a credit history maintained by a credit bureau. A credit report may not include all the information in a credit file.

credit history. Another term for the information on a credit report. A credit history is a record of how a person has repaid their credit obligations in the past.

credit limit. The total amount a company will allow a person to charge to a credit card or credit line. It's best for your credit score to keep your credit card balances below 35 percent of your credit limit. If you spend more than your credit limit, you will be charged an over-limit penalty anywhere from $10 to $50.

credit obligation. An agreement in which a person becomes legally responsible for paying back borrowed money.

credit repair. A generally unscrupulous or illegal form of credit counseling that promises the impossible, such as erasing accurate records from a credit report.

credit report. The individual records of a consumer's financial behavior kept by credit bureaus and provided to businesses when they want to evaluate potential borrowers. Credit reports include a consumer's name, current and former addresses, employment, credit and loan histories, inquiries, collection records, and public records such as bankruptcy filings and tax liens. Every adult can get one free report each year from each of the big three CRAs—Experian, Equifax, and TransUnion—at AnnualCreditReport.com.

credit-reporting agency. See *credit bureaus.*

credit score. A numerical evaluation of a person's credit history expressed as a three-digit number used by businesses to quickly understand how risky a borrower is. Credit scores are calculated using complex mathematical formulas that look at a person's most current payment history, debts, credit history, inquiries, and other factors from their credit report. Credit scores usually range from 300 to 850, with 680 or higher considered a "good" credit score. There are thousands of slightly different credit-scoring formulas (including FICO, beacon, and empirica scores) used by bankers, lenders, creditors, insurers, and retailers. Scores can vary based on how the formula evaluates credit data.

debt. The amount of money owed.

debt consolidation. A process of combining debts into one loan or repayment plan. Debt consolidation can be done on one's own, with a financial institution, or through a counseling service. Student loans are often consolidated in order to secure a lower interest rate. See also *debt counseling* and *debt settlement.*

debt counseling. A type of credit counseling that focuses specifically on helping people with debt issues. Instead of consolidating debts into one loan, debt counseling agencies negotiate with creditors using preset agreements and spread payments over a longer period in order to reduce the monthly amount due. Usually nonprofit companies, most of these agencies offer helpful and affordable services. Consumers should be aware that there are also debt counseling agencies that are expensive, ineffective, and even damaging to a client's credit score. See also *credit repair*.

debt settlement. A process in which a person pays an agency to negotiate directly with their creditors in the hopes of making significantly reduced settlements for their debts. Working with a debt settlement company can result in damaged credit from numerous late payments and collection records. Consumers should fully investigate the practices, reputation, and costs of working with a debt settlement company before signing up because nearly all of these companies are scams.

debt-to-available-credit ratio. The amount of money a person owes in outstanding debts compared to the total amount of credit they have available through all credit cards and credit lines. This ratio measures how much of their available credit they are using. The higher the debt-to-available-credit ratio, the more risky a person appears to potential lenders.

debt-to-income ratio. The percentage of monthly pretax income that is used to pay off debts such as auto loans, student loans, and credit card balances. Lenders look at two ratios: The front-end ratio is the percentage of monthly pretax earnings that is spent on house payments. In the back-end ratio, the borrower's other debts are factored in along with the house payments.

default. The status of a debt account that has not been paid. Accounts are usually listed as being in default after they have been reported late (delinquent) several times. A default is a serious negative item on a credit report.

delinquency. A term used for late payment or lack of payment on a loan, debt, or credit card account. Accounts are usually referred to as 30, 60, 90, or 120 days delinquent because most lenders have monthly payment cycles. A delinquency remains on a credit report for seven years and is damaging to a credit score.

demand draft checks. A type of electronic check that can be created online by entering account numbers listed on the bottom of a personal check and that can be cashed without a signature. This system was originally designed to help telemarketers take check payments over the phone. Now it is one of the fastest-growing fraud tools.

dispute. The process of submitting a request to the credit bureaus to have an error on a credit report corrected. Disputes are investigated and updates made to a credit report over a thirty-day period. If a correction is made, you will receive a letter from the credit bureaus and a copy of your updated credit report. If your dispute is rejected, you will receive a letter explaining why the credit bureaus could not verify the correction.

empirica score. A specific credit score developed by TransUnion. There are thousands of slightly different credit-scoring formulas used by bankers, lenders, creditors, insurers, and retailers. Scores can vary based on how the formula evaluates credit data.

Equal Credit Opportunity Act (ECOA). A law that protects consumers from discrimination on the basis of race, sex, public assistance income, age, marital status, nationality, or religion in the credit and lending process.

Equifax. One of the three national credit bureaus (also known as credit-reporting agencies) that collects and provides consumer financial records. See AnnualCreditReport.com to get one free copy every twelve months.

equity. The fair market value of a home minus the unpaid mortgage principal and liens. You build up equity in a home as you pay down your mortgage and as the property value increases. Also called lendable value or net value.

Experian. One of the three national credit bureaus that collects and provides consumer financial records. See AnnualCreditReport.com to get one free copy every twelve months.

expiration term. The set number of years that a record will remain on a credit report as mandated by the Fair Credit Reporting Act. Most negative records stay on a credit report for seven to ten years. The shortest expiration term is two years for inquiry records. The longest expiration term is fifteen years for paid tax liens or indefinitely for unpaid tax liens. Positive information can also stay on a credit report indefinitely.

Fair and Accurate Credit Transaction (FACT) Act. The FACT Act was signed into law December 2003 and includes several consumer credit industry regulations. This law requires credit bureaus to provide all United States residents with a free copy of their credit report once every twelve months. The law also includes new privacy regulations, identity theft protections, and dispute procedure requirements.

Fair Credit Reporting Act (FCRA). A federal law first passed in the 1970s that promotes accuracy, confidentiality, and proper use of information in the files kept by credit-reporting agencies. This law specifies the expiration terms of records on a credit report, defines who can access credit data, and grants consumers the right to view and dispute their credit records. This act is available online at FTC.gov.

Fannie Mae. The largest mortgage investor. A government-sponsored enterprise that buys mortgages from lenders, bundles them into investments, and sells them on the secondary mortgage market. Formerly known as the Federal National Mortgage Association.

Federal Housing Administration (FHA). A division of the Department of Housing and Urban Development (HUD) that provides mortgage insurance and sets construction and underwriting standards.

FICO score. A specific credit score developed by Fair Isaac Corporation. There are thousands of slightly different credit-scoring formulas used by bankers, lenders, creditors, insurers, and retailers. Scores can vary based on how the formula evaluates credit data.

file freeze. Residents of select states (currently California, Louisiana, Texas, Vermont, and Washington) can request that the credit bureaus freeze their credit reports. This freeze stops new credit from being issued in their name by blocking creditors, lenders, insurers, and other companies from accessing their credit data. In some cases, a $10 fee for each credit bureau is required to process the file freeze. The freeze can also be temporarily or permanently undone for an additional fee.

finance charge. The total cost of using credit. Besides interest charges, the finance charge may include other costs, such as cash-advance fees.

first mortgage. The primary loan on a real estate property. This loan has priority over all other "secondary" loans.

fixed rate. An interest rate for a credit card or loan that remains constant.

fixed rate mortgage (FRM). A mortgage with an interest rate that remains constant for the entire duration of the loan. FRMs have longer terms (fifteen to thirty years) and higher interest rates than adjustable rate mortgages but are not at risk for changing interest rates.

fixed rate option. A home equity line of credit financing option that allows borrowers to specify the payments and interest on a portion of their balance. This can be done a few times during the life of the loan, usually for an additional fee.

foreclosure. When a borrower is in default on a loan or mortgage, the creditor can enact a legal process to claim ownership of the collateral property. Foreclosure usually involves a forced sale of the property in which the proceeds go toward paying off the debt.

fraud alert. If you suspect that you are a victim of identity theft, you may contact the credit bureaus to request that a ninety-day fraud alert be placed on your credit reports. This alert notifies potential creditors to take extra steps to verify your identity before opening a new account. If you have been a victim of identity theft, you need to contact only one bureau to have a temporary ninety-day alert added to all three of your credit reports. If it turns out that your identity has been stolen, you can request an extended seven-year alert by providing documentation of the crime (such as a police report). There is also a special one-year fraud alert available for military personnel on active duty.

Freddie Mac. A government-sponsored firm that buys mortgages from lenders, pools them with other loans, and sells them to investors. Formerly known as the Federal Home Loan Mortgage Corporation.

front-end ratio or front ratio. A calculation of the percentage of monthly pretax income that goes toward a house payment. The general rule is that the front ratio should not exceed 28 percent.

garnishment. When a creditor receives legal permission to take a portion of a person's assets (bank account, salary, etc.) to repay a delinquent debt.

Ginnie Mae. A part of the Department of Housing and Urban Development (HUD) that buys mortgages from lending institutions and pools them to form securities, which it then sells to investors. Also known as the Government National Mortgage Association.

grace period. A period of time, often about twenty-five days, during which you can pay your credit card bill without incurring a finance charge. With most credit card accounts, the grace period applies only if you pay your balance in full each month. It does not apply if you carry a balance forward or in the case of cash advances. If your account has no grace period, interest will be charged on a purchase as soon as it is made.

high-LTV equity loan. A specific kind of home loan that causes a loan-to-value ratio to be 125 percent or more. When the total principal of a loan leaves the borrower with debt that exceeds the fair market value of the home, the interest paid on the portion of the loan above that value may not be tax deductible.

home equity. The part of a home's value that the mortgage borrower owns outright. This is the difference between the fair market value of the home and the principal balances of all mortgage loans.

home equity line of credit (HELOC). An open-ended loan that is backed by the part of a home's value that the borrower owns outright. This type of loan is used much like a credit card. Home equity lines of credit can be effective ways to borrow large sums of money with a relatively low interest rate. These types of loans should be used with caution. If borrowers are unable to repay the loan for some reason (loss of job, illness, etc.), they risk losing the home they used as collateral.

home equity loan (HEL). A loan that is backed by part of a home's equity. The entire amount is received by the borrower in a single payout with interest paid monthly on the outstanding balance (unlike a HELOC in which the borrower draws on the amount approved, as needed, and pays interest only on the amount drawn).

Home Ownership and Equity Protection Act. A law designed to discourage predatory lending in mortgages and home equity loans.

housing expense ratio. The percentage of monthly pretax income that goes toward a house payment. The general rule is that this ratio should not exceed 28 percent. This is also known as the "front ratio."

income verification. Loan applications may require fully documented proof of an applicant's income. Loans of this type usually offer lower interest rates than no-income or "no-doc" verification loans.

inquiry. An item on a credit report that shows that someone with a "permissible purpose" under FCRA regulations has requested a copy of credit report data. See also *promotional inquiry* and *soft inquiry*.

installment account. A type of loan in which the borrower makes the same payment each month. This includes personal loans and automobile loans. Mortgage loans are also installment accounts but are usually classified by the credit-reporting system as real estate accounts instead.

interest. The money a borrower pays for the ability to borrow from a lender or creditor. Interest is calculated as a percentage of the money borrowed and is paid over a specified time.

interest-only loan. A type of loan in which the repayment covers only the interest that accumulates on the loan balance and not the actual price of the property. The principal does not decrease with the payments. Interest-only loans usually have a term of one to five years, after which the entire principal becomes due and payable.

interest rate. A measure of the cost of credit, expressed as a percentage. For variable rate credit card plans, the interest rate is explicitly tied to another interest rate. The interest rate on fixed rate credit card plans, though not explicitly tied to changes in other interest rates, can also change over time.

interest rate cap. A limit on how much a borrower's percentage rate can increase or decrease at rate adjustment periods and over the life of the loan. Interest rate caps are used for ARM loans in which the rates can vary at certain points.

introductory rate. A temporary, low interest rate offered on a credit card in order to attract customers. This low rate usually lasts for about six months before converting to a normal fixed or variable rate. With some offers, the introductory rate can be revoked or terminated early if a person makes a late payment or violates some other terms of the account.

joint account. An account shared by two or more people. Each person on the account is legally responsible for the debt, and the account will be reported to each person's credit report.

judgment. A decision from a judge on a civil action or lawsuit; usually an amount of money a person is required to pay to satisfy a debt or as a penalty. Judgment records remain on a credit report for seven years and harm a credit score significantly.

jumbo mortgage. A loan that exceeds the limits set by Fannie Mae and Freddie Mac (usually when the loan amount is more than $200,000 to $400,000). Also known as a nonconventional or nonconforming loan, these mortgages usually have higher interest rates than standard loans.

late payment. A delinquent payment or failure to deliver a loan or debt payment on or before the time agreed. Late payments harm a credit score for up to seven years and are usually penalized with late payment charges.

late payment charge. A fee charged by a creditor or lender when a credit card payment is made after the date due. Late payment charges typically run from $25 to $50 per occurrence, regardless of the amount owed. Late fees on mortgages and installment loans are typically less harsh than those for open-ended accounts.

lender. The individual or financial institution who provides the loan.

lien. A legal claim against a person's property, such as a car or a house, as security for a debt. A lien (pronounced "lean") may be placed by a contractor who did work on a house or a mechanic who repaired a car and didn't get paid. The property cannot be sold without paying the lien. Tax liens can remain on a credit report indefinitely if left unpaid or for fifteen years from the date paid.

loan origination fee. A fee charged by a lender for underwriting a loan. The fee often is expressed in "points"; a point is 1 percent of the loan amount.

loan processing fee. A fee charged by a lender for accepting a loan application and gathering the supporting paperwork, usually about $300.

loan-to-value ratio (LTV). The percentage of a home's price that is financed with a loan. On a $100,000 house, if the buyer makes a $20,000 down payment and borrows $80,000, the loan-to-value ratio is 80 percent. When refinancing a mortgage, the LTV ratio is calculated using the appraised value of the home, not the sale price. You will usually get the best deal if your LTV ratio is below 80 percent.

low-documentation loan. A mortgage that requires less income and/or assets verification than a conventional loan. Low-documentation loans are designed for entrepreneurs or self-employed borrowers—or for borrowers who cannot or choose not to reveal information about their incomes.

low-down mortgage. A secured loan that requires a small down payment, usually less than 10 percent. Often, a low-down mortgage is offered to special kinds of borrowers such as first-time buyers, police officers, veterans, etc. These kinds of loans sometimes require the borrower to purchase mortgage insurance.

maxed out. A slang term for using up the entire credit limit on a credit card or a line of credit. Borrowing the maximum limit on cards or equity lines hurts a person's credit score.

merged credit report. Also called a 3-in-1 credit report, this type of report shows credit data from TransUnion, Equifax, and Experian in a side-by-side format for easy comparison. You will pay a fee to get this. Free reports required by law are available only at AnnualCreditReport.com.

minimum payment. The minimum amount that a credit card company requires a person to pay toward their debt each month, usually 3 to 4 percent of the outstanding balance or not less than $10.

mortgage banker. A person or company that originates home loans, sells them to investors, and processes monthly payments.

mortgage broker. A person or company that matches lenders with borrowers who meet their criteria. A mortgage broker does not make the loan directly like a mortgage banker but receives payment for their services.

mortgage refinance. The process of paying off and replacing an old loan with a new mortgage. Borrowers usually choose to refinance a mortgage to get a lower interest rate, lower their monthly payments, avoid a balloon payment, or take cash out of their equity.

mutual fund. Also called a "stock mutual fund," this is simply a fund that owns dozens, if not hundreds, of individual stocks. A mutual fund provides instant diversification. A person buys shares of a mutual fund, and each share gives them a stake in all the stocks owned by the fund.

negative amortization. This occurs when a minimum payment toward a debt is not enough to cover the interest charges. The debt balance continues to increase despite the payment.

no-documentation loan. A loan in which an applicant provides only the minimum information—name, address, and Social Security number. The underwriter decides on the loan based only on the applicant's credit history, the appraised value of the house, and the size of the down payment. This type of loan, also called a "stated income" loan, usually has higher interest rates than a standard loan.

opt-out. You can opt out from preapproved credit card offers, insurance offers, and other third-party marketing by calling 1-888-5-OPT-OUT. Calling this number will stop mail offers that use your credit data from all three credit bureaus. You can also call this number to ask to opt-in again.

over-limit fee. A fee, usually $10 to $50, charged by a creditor when spending exceeds the credit limit set on a card.

213

penalty rate. Also called "default rate," a higher interest rate applied to a credit card account if the account holder is late making payments.

periodic rate. The interest rate charged each billing period. For most credit cards, the periodic rate is a monthly rate. You can calculate your card's periodic rate by dividing the APR by 12. A credit card with an 18 percent APR has a monthly periodic rate of 1.5 percent.

PITI. Acronym for the four elements of a mortgage payment: principal, interest, taxes, and insurance.

point. A unit for measuring fees related to a loan; a point equals 1 percent of a mortgage loan. Some lenders charge "origination points" to cover the expense of making a loan. Some borrowers pay "discount points" to reduce the loan's interest rate.

preapproval letter. A document from a lender or broker that estimates how much a potential home buyer could borrow based on current interest rates and a preliminary look at credit history. The letter is not a binding agreement with a lender. Having a preapproval letter can make it easier to shop for a home and negotiate with sellers. It is better to have a pre-approval letter than an informal prequalification letter.

preapproved. A preapproved credit card offer means that a potential customer has passed a preliminary credit information screening. A credit card company can spurn a preapproved customer if it doesn't like the applicant's credit rating.

prepayment penalty. A fee that a lender charges a borrower who pays off a loan before the end of its scheduled term. Prepayment penalties are not charged by most standard lenders. Subprime borrowers should review the terms of their loan offers carefully to see if this fee is included.

principal. The amount of money borrowed or the amount of money owed, excluding interest.

private mortgage insurance (PMI). A form of insurance that protects a lender by paying the costs of foreclosing on a house if the borrower stops paying the loan. Private mortgage insurance usually is required if the down payment is less than 20 percent of the sale price.

promotional inquiry. A type of soft inquiry made by a creditor, lender, or insurer in order to send a person a preapproved offer. Only limited credit data is made available for this type of inquiry, and it does not harm a credit score.

public records. Information that is available to any member of the public. Public records such as a bankruptcy, tax lien, foreclosure, court judgment, or overdue child support harm a credit report and a credit score significantly.

qualifying ratios. As calculated by lenders, the percentage of income that is spent on housing debt and combined household debt.

rate shopping. Applying for credit with several lenders to find the best interest rate, usually for a mortgage or a car loan. If done within a short period of time, such as two weeks, it should have little impact on a person's credit score.

re-aging accounts. A process in which a creditor can roll back an account record with the credit bureaus. This is commonly used when cardholders request that late payment records be removed because they are incorrect or resulted from a special circumstance. However, re-aging can also be used illegally by collection agencies to make a debt account appear much younger than it actually is. Some collection agencies use this tactic to keep an account from expiring from a credit report in order to try to get a person to pay the debt.

repayment period. The period of a loan when a borrower is required to make payments. It usually applies to home equity lines of credit. During the repayment period, the borrower cannot take out any more money and must pay down the loan.

repossession. When a loan is significantly overdue, a creditor can claim property (cars, boats, equipment, etc.) that was used as collateral for the debt.

reverse mortgage. A mortgage that allows elderly borrowers to access their equity without selling their home. The lender makes payments to the borrower with a reverse mortgage. The loan is repaid from the proceeds of the estate when the borrower moves or passes away.

revolving account. An account in which a balance and monthly payment can fluctuate. Most credit cards are revolving accounts.

rewards card. A credit card that rewards spending with points, cash back programs, or airline miles. These types of cards usually require borrowers to have good credit and sometimes involve an annual fee.

risk score. Another term for a credit score. See also *beacon score, credit score, empirica score,* and *FICO score.*

Schumer Box. An easy-to-use chart that explains the rates, fees, terms, and conditions of a credit account. Creditors are required to provide this on credit applications by the U.S. Truth in Lending Act, and it usually appears on statements and other documents.

scoring model. A complex mathematical formula that evaluates financial data to predict a borrower's future behavior. There are thousands of slightly different scoring models used to generate credit scores.

second mortgage. A loan using a home's equity as collateral. A first mortgage must be repaid before a second mortgage in a sale.

secured credit card. A consumer credit account that requires the borrower to produce some form of collateral—usually a cash deposit equal to the amount of the credit limit on the card. Secured credit cards are easier to obtain than standard credit cards and are helpful for borrowers with poor credit or no credit.

secured debt. A loan that requires a piece of property (such as a house or a car) be used as collateral. This collateral provides security for the lender, since the property can be seized and sold if the borrower doesn't repay the debt.

settlement. An agreement reached with a creditor to pay a debt for less than the total amount due. Settlements can be noted on a credit report and are not as beneficial to one's credit as paying a debt in full.

Social Security Number (SSN). This unique nine-digit number is meant to track Social Security savings but is also used by creditors, lenders, banks, insurers, hospitals, employers, and numerous other businesses to identify a person's accounts. People who do not have a SSN, such as non-US citizens, use a nine-digit Individual Taxpayer Identification Number (ITIN) instead.

soft inquiry. A type of inquiry that does not harm a credit score. Soft inquiries are recorded when a business accesses a person's credit data for a purpose other than an application for credit. Soft inquiries include a request to see your own credit report and employment-related requests. This type of inquiry is recorded by the credit bureaus but does not usually appear on a credit report purchased by you or a business.

stock. A share of ownership in a company. Owners of stock receive part of the company's profits—and bear some of its losses—up to the amount of money they put into the stock.

subprime borrower. A borrower who does not meet the qualifications for standard credit and loan offers. Usually a subprime borrower has poor credit (a score under 650) due to late payments, collection accounts, or public records. Subprime borrowers can qualify for loans and credit but usually at a higher interest rate or with special terms.

teaser rate. Often called the introductory rate, it is the below-market interest rate offered to entice customers to switch credit cards or lenders.

TransUnion. One of the three national credit bureaus that collects and provides consumer financial records. See AnnualCreditReport.com to get one free copy every twelve months.

TRW. A former credit-reporting agency that is now part of Experian.

unsecured debt. A loan on which there is no collateral. Most credit card accounts are unsecured debt.

utilization ratio. The ratio between the credit limits on a person's accounts and the outstanding balances. This ratio shows lenders how much of one's available credit a person is using overall.

variable rate. A type of adjustable rate loan tied directly to the movement of some other economic index. For example, a variable rate might be prime rate plus 3 percent; it will adjust as the prime rate changes.

Mary Hunt, award-winning and bestselling author, syndicated columnist, and sought-after motivational speaker, has created a global platform that is making strides to help men and women battle the epidemic impact of consumer debt. Mary is the founder of Debt-Proof Living, a highly regarded organization consisting of an interactive website, a monthly newsletter, a daily syndicated column, and hundreds of thousands of loyal followers. Since 1992, DPL has been dedicated to its mission to provide hope, help, and realistic solutions for individuals who are committed to financially responsible and debt-free living.

As a speaker, Mary travels extensively, addressing conferences, corporations, colleges, universities, and churches at home and abroad. A frequent guest on radio and television, she has appeared on dozens of television shows, including *Dr. Phil*, *Good Morning America*, *The Oprah Winfrey Show*, and *Dateline*.

Mary lives with her husband in Colorado.

"*I would have had no idea where to start if I had not read this book.*"
—Denise J.

"Debt-Proof Living *was our salvation,
and now it is our daily living reference.*"
—Kathy W.

"*Because of* Debt-Proof Living *I have completely
changed my thinking about money.*"
—M. J.

"*You have changed my life.*"
—Beth G.

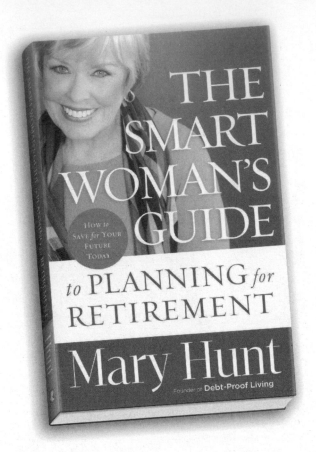

"Mary Hunt takes the fear out of
an often-terrifying topic. Any woman
who's ever wanted to be able to retire
confidently can benefit from the
down-to-earth knowledge in this book."

—Liz Pulliam Weston, *MSN Money* columnist and author of
The 10 Commandments of Money

"Simple rules of the road that cut through confusion, mystery, and misery."

—Lisa Rose, founder, First Friday Women

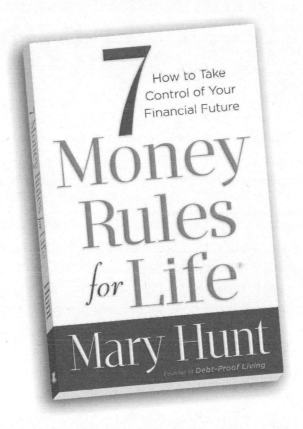

Mary Hunt, nationally syndicated financial columnist and founder of Debt-Proof Living, distills over 20 years of experience into seven simple principles that help people get out of debt and manage their money.

Revell
a division of Baker Publishing Group
www.RevellBooks.com

Available Wherever Books Are Sold
Also Available in Ebook Format